CAMBRIDGE LIBRARY COLLECTION

Books of enduring scholarly value

Women's Writing

The later twentieth century saw a huge wave of academic interest in women's writing, which led to the rediscovery of neglected works from a wide range of genres, periods and languages. Many books that were immensely popular and influential in their own day are now studied again, both for their own sake and for what they reveal about the social, political and cultural conditions of their time. A pioneering resource in this area is Orlando: Women's Writing in the British Isles from the Beginnings to the Present (http://orlando.cambridge.org), which provides entries on authors' lives and writing careers, contextual material, timelines, sets of internal links, and bibliographies. Its editors have made a major contribution to the selection of the works reissued in this series within the Cambridge Library Collection, which focuses on non-fiction publications by women on a wide range of subjects from astronomy to biography, music to political economy, and education to prison reform.

British Freewomen

Charlotte Carmichael Stopes (1841–1929) was a British scholar, a prolific writer and supporter of feminist causes. After becoming the first women to gain a Certificate of Arts in Scotland, Stopes published widely on Shakespeare and social reform, receiving an award from the British Academy in 1916 for her contributions to Shakespearian literary research. This volume, now reissued from the 1907 third edition, was first published in 1894. It contains Stopes' investigation into the history of British women's legal and civic rights. Through an analysis of state papers, parliamentary records and scholarly works on legal history, Stopes provides numerous historical examples of women holding extensive constitutional and legal rights, which are arranged according to the holder's social status. This pioneering feminist history became a key text used by women's suffrage activists to justify their position. For more information on this author, see http://orlando.cambridge.org/public/svPeople?person_id=stopch

Cambridge University Press has long been a pioneer in the reissuing of out-of-print titles from its own backlist, producing digital reprints of books that are still sought after by scholars and students but could not be reprinted economically using traditional technology. The Cambridge Library Collection extends this activity to a wider range of books which are still of importance to researchers and professionals, either for the source material they contain, or as landmarks in the history of their academic discipline.

Drawing from the world-renowned collections in the Cambridge University Library, and guided by the advice of experts in each subject area, Cambridge University Press is using state-of-the-art scanning machines in its own Printing House to capture the content of each book selected for inclusion. The files are processed to give a consistently clear, crisp image, and the books finished to the high quality standard for which the Press is recognised around the world. The latest print-on-demand technology ensures that the books will remain available indefinitely, and that orders for single or multiple copies can quickly be supplied.

The Cambridge Library Collection will bring back to life books of enduring scholarly value (including out-of-copyright works originally issued by other publishers) across a wide range of disciplines in the humanities and social sciences and in science and technology.

British Freewomen

Their Historical Privilege

CHARLOTTE CARMICHAEL STOPES

CAMBRIDGE UNIVERSITY PRESS

Cambridge, New York, Melbourne, Madrid, Cape Town, Singapore,
São Paolo, Delhi, Dubai, Tokyo, Mexico City

Published in the United States of America by Cambridge University Press, New York

www.cambridge.org
Information on this title: www.cambridge.org/9781108021968

© in this compilation Cambridge University Press 2010

This edition first published 1907
This digitally printed version 2010

ISBN 978-1-108-02196-8 Paperback

BRITISH FREEWOMEN

THEIR HISTORICAL PRIVILEGE

BY

CHARLOTTE CARMICHAEL STOPES

DIPLOMEE, EDIN. UNIVERSITY

Author of " Shakespeare's Family," " Shakespeare's Warwickshire's Contemporaries," " The Sphere of ' Man,' " etc.

" I do own for myself what Seneca the Declaimer saith, that I take pleasure in going back to studies of antiquity, and in looking behind me to our grandsires' better times."

As saith an old Latin poet :

> " Antique, buried in rubbish, old and musty,
> Which make one verst in customs old and new,
> And of Laws, Gods, and Men giving a view,
> Render the careful student skilled and trusty."
>
> *Inner Temple*, Dec. 25, 1610.

Author's Preface of John Selden's " Janus Anglorum," translated by Redman Westcot, *alias* Littleton.

LONDON

SWAN SONNENSCHEIN & CO., LIM.

NEW YORK : CHARLES SCRIBNER'S SONS

1907

Firi st Edition, *May* 1894; Second Edition, *July* 1894.
Third Edition, *October* 1907.

CONTENTS

PREFACE

IN the spring of 1885, when planning to attend the British Association meeting in Aberdeen that summer, it struck me that I might prepare a paper on a Woman's Subject, and try to find an opportunity of reading it before the Section of Economics and Statistics there. The paper divided itself into two, which I carefully entitled—I. The History and Statistics of Woman's Privilege; and II. The Economic Effects of the Abstention of Women from Voting.

They were, as might have been expected, both rejected. I was told that, though they formed valuable contributions to Constitutional History, the Committee felt they would certainly lead to political discussion, which must not be risked. At a public meeting in Aberdeen the same week, I gave a resumé of my arguments, and the materials then collected I have frequently used since in Drawing-room Addresses, and in private conversation ; in public papers, and in friendly correspondence. So many have been surprised at the facts, and interested in the results, that, at the present crisis, I thought it advisable to spend another six months in careful verification of details, and in grouping apparently disconnected data, so that their full import might be seen at a glance. My first authorities were Sydney Smith's "Enfranchisement of Woman the Law of the Land" (1876), and Mr. Chisholm Anstey's Book and Papers on "The Representation of the People's Act" (1876).

Thence I went through the materials of Constitutional History, the Statutes, Rolls of Parliament, State Papers, Parliamentary Writs, Journals of the House of Commons, Reports of Cases, Works on Law, History, and Archæology, both printed and manuscript.

Just as my paper was complete enough for the purpose

in hand, M. Ostrogorski's book upon "Women's Rights"
appeared. But he had considered the question in regard to
all women, I only in regard to British Freewomen. He
was the more general, I the more special, and I had noted
several points which had escaped him in regard to the prime
question of the day.

I consulted Miss Helen Blackburn, Editor of the *Englishwoman's Review*, and she urged me to bring out what I had
prepared. She had always thought the work necessary, had
intended to undertake it herself, when she could find leisure,
and thought that now was the most fitting time to publish.

She generously placed her note-books at my disposal,
whence I have gleaned many interesting facts in support of
my own. Therefore this little book may be taken as her
voice as well as mine. The points I specially wish to be
considered, are :—

1st, The Ethnological.—The racial characteristics of our
ancestors. They reverenced women.

2nd, The Philological. —All old Statutes are couched in
general terms. Through a deficiency in the English
language, the word "man" is a common term, including
woman as well as man, even by Statute.

3rd, The Legal.—The late Laureate speaks of the liberties of men as broadening down from precedent to precedent.
We find that the liberties of women have, on the other
hand, been narrowed down from precedent to precedent.
Sir Edward Coke, the technical cause of this limitation, is
only a fellow-mortal, liable to error.

4th, The Historical, in which facts speak for themselves.

5th, The Biblical, in which prejudice and mistranslation
have confused the ideas of readers on this point. Some may
disagree with my conclusions, but I trust they may accept
the facts, and do what they can with them.

No one can deny that it is *just* to grant women the
Suffrage, no one can deny that it would be *advantageous
for them* to receive it. There is no reason that a thing
should be because it has been, but when the only objection

brought against a thing is, that it has not been, it is time to test if that statement be really true. We have not found the received assertions true in regard to this subject. Hence the publication of this little book.

Thus far I had written as Preface to the little Brochure that I printed for the use of the Women's Suffrage Societies a month ago. But as the whole Thousand was ordered before it came from the printers, it was evident that I ought to publish my work formally, with the many additions I had held back from lack of space, and with the article from the *Athenæum*, No. 3475, which I had been permitted to incorporate. Amongst the labour-saving appliances of the day, may be classified collections of verified facts. I trust these may reach the hands of those for whom I write, *brave women* and *fair men*.

CHARLOTTE CARMICHAEL STOPES.

6th June, 1894.

PREFACE TO THE THIRD EDITION

TWO editions of this little work followed each other very closely in 1894, and a third one has now been called for, from the increasing interest in the subject. It is the only work which has attempted to collect and classify the references to the privileges of women in the past, and has applied them to the needs of the present.

To this edition I have added a much-needed index, which was only omitted before, because of the work being hurried through the press in order to be sent by Miss Blackburn to the members of the House, before the discussion of that year. I am glad to say I have been able to cut out all but a reference to "Women and the Universities," as changes have made it unnecessary. I have included a good many additional examples, and have brought the history of our fortunes up to date in the "Conclusion."

The reviews of my earlier editions were in general favourable, but I was somewhat criticised for incomplete references. The fact was, that when I had once given the reference, I did not repeat it every time I mentioned the same case. This I have done now. I was also checked for a reference to "The Statutes of the Realm," vol. i., p. 220. But that has been upheld by the highest authority. "The Statutes of the Realm" is the official title of the special publication, presented in 1810 by George III. to the Houses of Parliament. It may be seen at page 220, vol. i., that there is no reign, and no regnal year attached. Reasons and authorities are given for a proximate date. But these cannot be given in the short space allowed to references. Those who wish to learn will generally find mine sufficient.

There was also one criticism of my transcripts. Classical scholars need not enter into the arena of discussions

concerning record Latin, French, or English, or attempt to
decide on the proper proportion of each without direct
comparison with original sources. Where these are even
hasty MSS., they must be followed, errors and all.

I have been able, however to correct the misprints which
arose from my having to confide proof-correcting to another.
These were only literals. For my real errors, which have
not been noted by any reviewer, and for my incompleteness,
of which I was painfully aware, I have now done my best by
careful study and revision of the whole. I must express a
great debt of gratitude for the kind help in this toil of Mr. C.
Pidduck, Solicitor, of Bowdon, near Manchester, who has
spared no trouble nor enthusiasm in trying to improve a
work, which he is pleased to consider important to the cause
of women, and unique in its place in Literature.

CHARLOTTE CARMICHAEL STOPES.

53 STANLEY GARDENS, N.W.,
August, 1907.

BRITISH FREEWOMEN

THEIR HISTORICAL PRIVILEGE

CHAPTER I

PRELIMINARY

ANCIENT HISTORY AND BRITISH WOMEN

"Let us look at the beginnings of things, for they help us to understand the ends."

THOUGH early British traditions may survive in later Literature, we cannot accept them for critical purposes. The century before the birth of Christ is the earliest date of our authentic history. The words of the Romans, strangers and enemies, however, give unexceptionable testimony. Nothing impressed the Romans more than the equality of the sexes among the Northern nations; the man's reverence for womanhood, the

A

woman's sympathy with manhood, and the high code
of morality that was the natural outcome of this well-
balanced society.

Plutarch ("De Virtutibus Mulierum") says: "Concerning the virtues of women, I am not of the same
mind with Thucydides.   For he would prove that
she is the best woman concerning whom there is
least discourse made by people abroad, either to her
praise or dispraise; judging that as the person, so
the very name of a good woman ought to be retired
and not to gad abroad.* . . . And seeing that many
worthy things, both public and private, have been
done by women, it is not amiss to give a brief historical
account of those that are public in the first place."
Among the examples he cites, there is that of the con-
tinental Celts, kindred to the British.   Some of these
wandered north-west, and some due south.   "There
arose a very grievous and irreconcilable contention
among the Celts before they passed over the Alps to
inhabit that tract of Italy which now they inhabit, which
proceeded to a civil war.   The women, placing themselves between the armies, took up the controversies,
argued them so accurately, and determined them so im-
partially that an admirable friendly correspondence and
general amity ensued, both civil and domestic.   Hence
the Celts made it their practice to take women into consultation about peace or war, and to use them as medi-
ates in any controversies that arose between them and

* Cited in Selden's "Epinomis," p. 6; his " Janus Anglorum," p. 24.

their allies. In the League, therefore, made with Hanni-
bal, the writing runs thus—If the Celts take occasion of
quarrelling with the Carthaginians, the governors and
generals of the Carthaginians in Spain shall decide the
dispute; but if the Carthaginians accuse the Celts, the
Celtic women shall decide the controversy." The Romans
were much struck by the similar position of women
among the Britons, Belgic and Celtic alike. Charles
Isaac Elton ("Origins of English History"), on
the authority of Ammianus Marcellinus, says of the
women, "that their approximation to the men in stature
was the best evidence that the nation had advanced out
of barbarism." Selden's "Janus Anglorum," or "The
English Janus," ed. 1683, c. xiii., has as heading,
"Women admitted to public debates. A large com-
mendation of the sex, together with a vindication of
their fitness to govern, against the Salick Law, made
out by several examples of most nations." Here Selden
shows what honour was paid to the counsels, the prudence,
the virtue of the Gaulish ladies, and refers to the passage
of Plutarch quoted above. "Cornelius Tacitus tells us
of the Britons that they were wont to war under the
conduct of women, and to make no difference of sex in
places of command and government, which places yet
there are some who stiffly deny that women by right
should have the charge of. . . . What did the Germans,
our ancestors? They thought there was in that sex
something of sanctity and foresight, nor did they slight
their counsels nor neglect the answers they gave when

questions were put to them about matters of business,
and as superstition increased, held most of them for
goddesses." . . . He elsewhere says of these: "Let us
more especially have to do with the Britons, as those
amongst whom are those choice and singular altars, not
anywhere else to be met with in the whole world,
with this inscription, Deis Matribus, To the Mother-
Goddesses." He also, in his chapter on "Women" in
the "Janus Anglorum," reminds us, that "Boadicea so
successfully commanded the British armies as to beat
and conquer the Roman Viceroy, and no doubt that
noble lady was a deliberative member of the Council
where the resolution was taken to fight, and that she
should command the forces." Tacitus ("Vita Agric.,"
c. xvi.) says: "Under the leadership of Boadicea, a
woman of kingly descent (for they admit of no
distinction of sex in their Royal successions), they all
rose to arms. Had not Paulinus, on hearing of
this outbreak, rendered · prompt succour, Britain would
have been lost." He owns elsewhere that had the
Britons but been able to unite among themselves, the
Romans could not have conquered them ; and he more
than once notes the bravery of the women in stimulating
the warriors.

More fully in his "Annals" (B. xiv.), Tacitus describes
how Suetonius Paulinus attacked Mona (Anglesea), the
stronghold of the Druids; and how the warlike priestesses
dashed about clothed in black, like furies, with dis-
hevelled hair, and with torches in their hands, encourag-

ing and threatening the soldiers, and when all was lost, perishing bravely among the flames kindled by the conqueror. This is told, not in the tones with which one belauds compatriot heroines, but in those of an enemy, to whom these women added new terrors and increased troubles. Meanwhile, in the East the Roman statue of Victory had fallen from its place in the temple of Claudius at Camalodunum, *i.e.*, Colchester, evil signs and omens weakened the hearts of the Roman soldiers, and frantic priestesses encouraged the hopes of the British force thereby. Boadicea, having succeeded in uniting some of the neighbouring tribes, had driven Catus over the sea, had subdued Petelius Cerialus, had destroyed the Colonia at Camalodunum, had sacked Verulam, and marched on London, building an intrenched camp near what we now call Islington. Suetonius Paulinus, fresh from the slaughter of the sacred Druid host, advanced to meet her. Tacitus describes the position of the armies, and reports her speech. Not being "unaccustomed to address the public," she called her army to witness "that it was usual for the Britons to war under the conduct of women, but on that occasion she entered the field, not as one descended from ancestors so illustrious to recover her kingdom and her treasure, but as one of the humblest among them, to take vengeance for liberty extinguished, her own body lacerated with stripes, and the chastity of her daughters defiled. . . . They would see that in that battle they must conquer or perish. Such was the fixed

resolve of a woman ; the men might live if they pleased and
be the slaves of the Romans." " Neither was Suetonius
silent at so perilous a juncture, for though he confided
in the bravery of his men, yet he mingled exhortations
with entreaties. ' In that great host were to be seen
more women than efficient men. Unwarlike, unarmed,
they would give way the instant they felt the sword and
valour of those victorious troops, etc.' " Then follows the
account of the battle. " The soldiers spared not even
the lives of the women, nay the very beasts, pierced
with darts, seemed to swell the heaps of the slain. The
glory gained that day was signal indeed, and equal to the
victories of ancient times, for there are authors who
record that of the Britons were slain almost 80,000, of
our men about 400, with not many more wounded "
(A.D. 61).

That Boadicea's defeat was gloried in as being such a
triumph to the Roman arms is in itself a witness to her
prowess. The numbers of the slain did not likely represent warriors alone. The carriages with their wives
and children lined the field. The Roman thought that
the defeated Britons *could not* fly past these. They
would not. Husbands, wives, and babes were slain
together, and reckoned together, perhaps the very beasts
of burden among the heaps of the slain were reckoned
too. Anything to increase the Roman " glory."

There is no picture more touching in the history of
our country ! The forces of oppression and lust, the
spirit of Nero himself, then Emperor, were ranged against

this woman. With superhuman energy, as patriot, as mother, and as *individual,* she struggled against these in defence of country, home, and honour. And *she failed !* Had circumstances been but slightly altered, had the brave Caractacus been but able to hold out a little longer, and take shelter with her, instead of trusting the rival Queen Cartismandua, how differently might our British history have read to-day.

Cartismandua was a Queen, too, in her own right, wedded freely to the neighbouring Prince Venutius, but nevertheless personally elected as the supreme ruler and leader of the united tribes of the Brigantes, making contracts and treaties for all. Caractacus, after his nine years' struggle, had fled for shelter and for help to her in the year 50 A.D. (*See* "Tacitus Annals," xiv., 36.) But as Elton says in his "Origins of English History," "she was far-seeing enough to see the hopelessness of contest with the Romans." Already Romanised in heart and spirit, she betrayed her countryman, cast off her husband, forfeited her honour, and finally lost the crown of her inheritance.

The blameless Boadicea suffered for her sins twelve years later, in that sad year of 62 A.D. That defeat rang the death-knell of the freedom of British womanhood, and of the spirit of British manhood. In such a crisis it is *not* the fittest who survive. They who lived to tread upon her grave were born of lower possibilities. Yet she *has lived,* the typal woman of the British past.

I know that I may be expected to speak of the Empress

Helena, claimed by Camalodunum (now Colchester) as the only daughter of its Coel II., the wife of Constantius, the mother of Constantine, the Christian convert, the finder of the true Cross. Good as she was, refined and cultivated too, she was, nevertheless, but a Romanised Briton, a Roman wife, a Roman mother, under Roman Law. And the Roman Law was a meaner foster-mother for feminine virtues than the free old British Law.

The withdrawal of the Roman troops for home affairs hastened a new crisis, in which the Britons, made limp by protection and an alien government, were unable to hold their own against invading tribes. No longer was the British wife the brave helpmeet, the counsellor, the inspirer of the British man. Roman customs had completed what the Roman arms and the Roman laws had begun, and the spirit of British Womanhood had no reserve force in itself to spare. Then came an infusion of new blood into the land, fortunately not of Latin race, but of a good northern stock, that reverenced woman still. Speaking of that stock in earlier times, Tacitus ("Germ.," c. viii.) says: "The women are the most revered witnesses of each man's conduct, and his most liberal applauders. To their mothers and their wives they bring their wounds for relief, who do not dread to count or search out the gashes. The women also administer food and encouragement to those who are fighting." "They even suppose somewhat of sanctity and prescience to be inherent in the female sex, and therefore neither despise their counsels nor disregard their responses. We have beheld, in the reign of Vespasian, Veleda, long reverenced by many as a deity. Aurinia, moreover, and several others, were formerly held in similar veneration, but not with a similar flattery, nor as though they had been goddesses" (c. xviii.). "Almost alone among barbarians they are content with one wife. . . . The wife does not bring a dower to the husband, but the husband to the wife, he brings no trinkets, but oxen, a horse, a shield, a spear, and a sword. . . . Lest the woman should think herself to stand apart from aspirations after noble deeds, and from the perils of war, she is reminded by the ceremony which inaugurates marriage (in which she is handed a spear) that she is her husband's partner in toil and danger, destined to suffer and to dare with him alike in peace and in war. . . ." "She must live and die with the feeling that she is receiving what she must hand down to her children, neither tarnished nor depreciated, what future daughters-in-law may receive, and may so pass on to her grandchildren" (c. xix.). "Thus with their virtue protected, they live uncorrupted by the allurements of public shows or the stimulant of feastings. Clandestine correspondence is equally unknown to men and women. The young men marry late, and their vigour is unimpaired. Nor are the maidens hurried into marriage. Well-matched and vigorous they wed, and the offspring reproduce the strength of their parents" (Church's Translation).

These racial peculiarities also marked the early Saxon

invaders, though there were no foreign witnesses to note them with surprise. The native writers took them too much as a matter of course to consider them worth noting. It is only indirectly that we can glean the state of affairs from public records. Samuel Heywood, in his "Ranks of the People among the Anglo-Saxons," says (p. 2): "The word Cwen originally signified a wife in general, but was by custom converted into a title for the wife of a king. . . . It was customary for Saxon monarchs to hold their courts with great solemnity three times a year. The Queen Consort, at these assemblies, wore her crown also, and was seated on a throne near the King. When an assembly of the nobles met at Winchester to adjust the complaints of the secular clergy against St. Dunstan, the King presided, having his Queen seated by his side" ("Eadmer de Vita St. Dunstan," Ang. Sacra., II., 219). . . .

"The Queen Consort had her separate household and attendants. . . ." "It is highly probable that in ancient as well as modern times the Queen Consort was considered as *feme sole* in all legal proceedings. Sir Edward Coke being called on to prove that this was the common law before the Conquest, produced a charter made by Ethelswurth, Queen of the Mercians, in the lifetime of her husband, giving away the lands in her own power, her husband being only an attesting witness. We find Queens Consort acting in all other respects as *femes soles* in tenure, management, and alienation of real property. Emma, Ethelred's Queen, gave a munificent grant to St. Swithins, Winchester. Alswythe, the Queen of King Alfred, began to erect a house for nuns at Winchester, finished by her son Edward. Queens attested their husbands' grants, and accorded their assents to acts done and engagements made. Queens Dowager were also present, and subscribed their names to Royal grants as being content with them " (Selden's " Epinomis," p. 3).

Though, of course, the Royal rank increased the woman's power, the law and custom for Queens was but the reflex of the common law and custom of the time for all women. Selden says: " Ladies of birth and quality sat in the Saxon Witenagemot," and Gurdon, in his " Antiquities of Parliament," vol. i., p. 164, adds: " Wightred, the next Saxon legislator, summoned his Witas to the Witenagemot at Berghamstead, where his laws were made with the advice and consent of his Witas (which is a *general* term for the nobility), for the laws were signed by the King, Werburg his Queen, the Bishops, Abbots, Abbesses, and the *rest* of the Witas " (*see* " Sax. Chron.,"48). In Spelman's " Concilia Britannica," p. 190, we find also that Wightred's council at Beconceld (694) included women, for the Queen and Abbesses signed the decisions along with the King and the Abbots (p. 192). The charter to Eabba the Abbess is granted by Wightred and his Queen (p. 486).

The charter to Glastonbury is signed, after the name of the King, " Ego Elfgiva ejusdem Regis Mater cum gaudio consensi " (p. 533). In the " Diploma Comiti, Regis Angliæ," after the King's name, " Ego Emma

Regina signo crucis confirmo." More may be learned
of this Queen by consulting Hardy's "Catalogue of
Authorities for the History of Great Britain," vol. iii.,
p. 2, Queen Emma.

The second charter of Edward the Confessor to St.
Peter's at Westminster contains not only the signature of
the sainted King, but " Ego Edgitha Regina huic dona-
tioni Regiæ consentiens subscripsi " (p. 631). And at
the council summoned to consider the Bull of Nicholas
the Pope to Edward the Confessor, after the King, signs
" Ego Edgitha Regina omni alacritate mentis hoc
corroboravi." The different expressions used show that
the signatures were no mere accident, no vapid formality.

In the council held to grant privileges to the Church,
" præsentibus etiam clarissimis Abbatissis, hoc est,
Hermehilda, Truinberga et Ataba reverenda, ut sub-
scriberent rogavi " (p. 198).

" King Edgar's charter to the Abbey of Crowland
(961) was signed with the consent of the nobles and
abbesses, for many abbesses were formerly summoned
to Parliament " (Plowden's " Jura Anglorum," p. 384.
Also William Camden's " Antiquity of Parliament ").

" Ego Ælfrith Regina " is the signature to the charter
that the King of Mercia grants to the Abbey of
Worcester. " Ethelswith Regina " subscribes with
Burghred, King of Mercia or Mercland, in the
Register of Worcester.

Edward the Confessor's charter to Agelwin is confirmed by his wife, " Ego Edgitha Regina consentio."

So in a charter of King Knut to the Abbey of St. Edmundesbury, his wife Alfgwa signs, "Ego Alfgifa Regina" (Selden's "Titles of Honour," 2nd edition, c. vi., p. 118).

There had been amid the Saxons, Queens Regnant as well as Queens Consort. William of Malmesbury writes in admiration of Sexburga, the Queen Dowager of Cenwalch, King of the West Saxons, 672 A.D., "that there was not wanting to this woman a great spirit to discharge the duties of the kingdom. She levied new armies, kept the old ones to duty, governed her subjects with clemency, kept her enemies quiet with threats—in a word, did everything at that rate that there was no other difference between her and any King in management except her sex" (Malmesbury, Gesta Regum Anglorum, Book I., c. ii. Translation by Dr. J. A. Giles, Bohn's Library, 1895, p. 30). Selden also writes in his "Epinomis," p. 3 : "Of the gynocracy of Martia, wife to King Guinthelin, a woman very learned." And again in his "Janus Anglorum," p. 7, he gives "A brief account of Queen Regent, Martia, widow to King Quinteline, who had undertaken the tuition of Sisillius, son to them both." Ethelfleda, too, the daughter of the great Alfred, called the Lady of Mercia, ruled that kingdom after the death of her father and her husband for eight years, and completed the work that her great father had begun in finally defeating and subjugating the intruding Danes.

There is also a curious notice of Queen Edith,

in "The Life and Times of Ralph Allen of Prior Park, Bath," by M. E. M. Peach, p. 22. "The Burgh of Bath, together with whatever pertained to it of Royal estate, came to the hands of King Edward at his accession . . . and he appears to have bestowed the whole upon his wife Edith. The estate thus passing from the Crown was subject to hidation, and so became geldable. On the other hand, it retained one great mark of Royalty. It continued to be a seat of high justice. Queen Edith herself exercised the function of High Justiciar. She paid the Tertius Denarius of the Crown Pleas of Bath to her brother Harold, while Earl of Somerset. She retained Bath and her office as High Justiciar after the Conquest. Surely it was in that capacity that, on 28th February, 1072, she presided in the Church of Wilton, over that memorable contract, whereby the Saxon Thane Alsor, sold the Somerset Manor of Combe to Giso, Bishop of Wells. . . . Such a transaction had no validity save by warranty of the King or his Vicegerent." Women landowners sat in the Shire Gemote, or held Motes of their own ; women burgesses were present at Folkmotes, or at Revemotes. In short, the privileges of women in the Saxon times were nearly equal to those they held in British times.

The Abbess Hilda presided over the monastery at Streneshalh, Whitby, where was a man's wing and a woman's wing, the Church coming between them. Among her disciples were educated many learned bishops. An ecclesiastical synod met at her abbey (664), at which she presided, that the calm of her presence and the influence of her control might soothe excitement on the vexed questions of the day, chiefly those regarding Easter. There were delegates from Rome, from the Scots, from the Angles and the Britons (*see* Bede's " Ecclesiastical History," lib. 3, c. xxv., and lib. 4, c. xxiii., xxiv.). Also Spelman's " Concilia" (p. 145) describes " Synodus Pharensis rogatu Hildæ illic Abbatissæ celebratæ." Spelman preserves also (p. 205) " Epistola Johannis Pa. VII.," to " Ethelredum Regem Merciorum." " Episcopus suo more obnitentibus beatissima virgo Elfleda soror Alfridi, Abbatissa post Hildam de Streneshalb, terminum negotio fixit dicens Dimissis ambagibus testamentum fratris mei, cui, præsens interfui, profero," etc. Other women held similar positions in England and in Scotland, as well as St. Bridget of the Abbey of Kildare in Ireland. The earliest British writer still extant, Gildas of Alcluid (now Dumbarton), reports the fact of women presiding over councils and abbeys without comment or surprise.

Holinshed, B. VI., c. ii., p. 142, follows Higden in the story of St. Modwenna, " a virgin in Ireland greatly renowned in the world, unto whom the forenamed King Ethelwolf sent his son Alfred to be cured of a disease that was thought incurable, but by her means he recovered health, and therefore, when her monastery was destroyed in Ireland, Modwen came over to England, unto whom King Ethelwolf gave land to build two abbeys and also delivered unto her his sister Edith,

to be professed a nun.   Modwen hereupon built two
monasteries, one at Poulesworth, joining to the bounds
of Arderne, wherein she placed the foresaid Edith, with
Osith and Athea; the other, whether it was a monastery
or cell, she founded in Streneshall or Trentshall, where
she herself remained solitary a certain time in prayer,
and other virtuous exercises.   And as it is reported, she
went thrice to Rome, and finally died, being 130 years of
age.   Many monasteries she builded both in England
and also in Scotland, as at Striveling and Edenborough,
and in Ireland also."   The Earl of Mercia built the
Abbey at Burton and transferred St. Modwen's bones
thither.   (*See* Gale's Annals, vol. iii., Book VI., p. 256 ;
Leland's Collectanea, vol. ii., p. 375.)

The Norman invaders swept like a whirlwind over
old institutions, yet some of the strongest stood firm.
They were, after all, of the same Church, and Church
and Cloister preserved the records of Saxon liberties
and the customs of Saxon times.   The clerical and lay
powers of many Abbesses were handed down unimpaired
to their successors in Norman times.   The conquest was
not one of extermination but of superposition.   The
great mass of the *people* remained Saxon in heart.   The
Normans were, too, of a kindred race, though they had
come from a long sojourn in a land where language,
thought, and custom had become Latinised, a land that
already held the principles of the Salic Law.   William
promised to respect the laws of the country, but there is
no appeal against a conqueror s will or a soldier's sword.

The lands they wrested from the Saxons, the Normans held of the King by Feudal Tenure and by Military Service. Their laws, customs, and language dominated the Saxons, as did their swords. But only for a time. The struggles with France formed, through a common antagonism, a united nation of the varying races in the island. To complete the union, the nation went back to the language of the Saxons, and, when opportunity for freedom called, went back to their old laws as a basis of the new. That women suffered more than men did from the Norman invasion might only have been expected. But that they did not do so nearly to the extent that it is commonly supposed, can be proved by reference to competent authorities, by whom the limitations of their privileges are shown to proceed on definite and comprehensible lines until comparatively modern times.

CHAPTER II

THE MODERN BASES OF PRIVILEGE

" All rights arise out of justice. . . . Justice is a constant and perpetual will to award to each his right. . . . Jurisprudence is the knowlege of divine and human things, the science of what is just and unjust."—BRACTON. DE LEGIBUS ANGLIÆ, Book I., c. iv.— "Of the division of things."—*Temp. Hen. III.*

THE relation between Property and Privilege has been the determining principle in Constitutional Evolution, and the distinction between the sexes in the matter of Property has been the radical cause of the distinction between them in regard to Privilege. It is necessary to trace this. The custom of Military Tenure made male heirs more valuable to the Crown than female heirs, inasmuch as personal service was more effective and reliable than representative service; and, therefore, in early Norman days, when all lands lay in the King's gift, he was eager to confirm each succeeding son of the last owner in his possessions before *any* of the daughters. But the principles of justice, the customs of the land, and the springs of human nature, combined in opposition to a further exercise of the Royal will, so that *all* the daughters succeeded before any of the collateral heirs, before uncle,

18

cousin, or nephew. Husbands and fathers would not have risked their lives freely in the King's wars, if they knew that wives and daughters were to lose their estates at the same time as they lost the protection of their strong right arms. A survival of Saxon opinion strangely affected further the position of daughters, when the chaos of custom took form in law. An eldest-born son could inherit to the detriment of his younger brothers, following the Norman custom of primogeniture, but the eldest-born daughter held no privilege over her younger sisters, who were all *co-parceners* with her as regarded the inheritance, in the manner that children of both sexes inherited among the Saxons, and among the representatives of the Saxons, the freemen of Kent. (*See* p. 43, post.) An indivisible inheritance, such as a title, fell in abeyance among daughters until decided by the selection of the Crown, though it was generally granted to the eldest daughter.* Unless a woman, therefore, was an only child, she did

---

* This custom was not clear among the Normans. In one well-known case at least, the younger sisters were made Abbesses, or otherwise disposed of, and the eldest made by the Norman law sole heir. Mabile, eldest daughter of Robert Fitzhaymo, was heir of all his lands, and King Henry I. wished to marry her to his illegitimate son Robert. This she long withstood, giving as her reason that she would not have a man for her husband that had not two names. When the King remedied that by calling his son Fitz Roy, she said, "That is a fair name as long as he shall live, but what of his son and his descendants?" The King then offered to make him Earl of Gloucester. "Sir," quoth the maiden, "then I like this well; on these terms I consent that all my lands shall be his." (Robert of Gloucester's "Brut," and Seyers' "Memoirs of Bristol," p. 353).

not succeed to the entire advantages of "the heir," but
as only child, and sole heiress, she inherited to the full
the rights and privileges of her father, brother, or ancestor.
Sex-in-itself did not *disqualify* a woman from anything.
There was no excusing a woman a duty, and *consequently*
no denying her a privilege. "*Essoin de servitio regis*
(excuse from the service of the King) lyeth not where
the party is a woman" (Statute 12, Ed. II.). The
only advantage granted her, that of "sending a deputy,"
she was allowed in common with men, frail or infirm, or
over the age of bearing arms.

The Feudal System has been credited with limiting
Personality and Privilege to males ; therefore it startles
some students of history to find that it was only on the
extinction of the Feudal System, and the translation of
service-payments into money-payments, that women lost
the definite place assigned to them. Women's rights
came second in Feudal Times, because they had to be
protected by men's swords; women's rights came no-
where in later times, when freedom towards property
would have made them able to protect themselves. The
encroachments naturally took place first in regard to
married women. In ancient times even a married
woman could be "free," both as an inheritor and as an
earner. In the very highest ranks she remained so. She
was free to contract, to sign, to seal, to act as a *feme sole*.
On her marriage she conferred her title on her husband,
as men did theirs upon their wives.* The lands were held

* " Both in England and in France, females originally communi-

in common. The responsibilities she could not undertake herself he fulfilled as her representative. When
she died he lost his representative character; his tenure
of her lands was only "by courtesy," and that only if he
had a child by her; if not, they reverted at her death to
the donor. (*See* "Statutes of the Realm," vol. i., p. 220.)
But a widow also could hold her husband's lands under
certain conditions, either by her marriage settlement,
her husband's will, or the King's gift, combined with the
right of Dower. Many examples of widows doing so
are given later. Even where there were heirs, and
her husband died intestate, a widow had a legal right
to the third part of her husband's property. In Kent
she had a right to the half till she married again, as a
man held the half of his wife's property till he married
again. (*See* "The Customal of Kent." *See* Bracton,
lib. v., cap. 30, f. 437[b]. Blackstone, Book II., c. viii.; 1
Steph. Com. 258, 12th edition.) In some districts by
"Borough English" she held the whole.

The Laws of Chivalry refined the Upper Classes,

cated their titles and dignities to their husbands. Many instances
of this are to be found in the arguments on the claim of Mr. Bertie
to the Barony of Willoughby. But this has long since ceased, and
we may apply to this circumstance the remark contained in the
former part of this work, respecting curtesy in titles of honour, that
from the late creations by which women have been made peeresses
in order that the issue of their husbands might have titles, yet the
husbands themselves continue commoners." (Hargrave's Note on
Coke upon Littleton, 326[a].)

Baroness Burdett-Coutts did not ennoble her husband; and
Benjamin D'Israeli (perhaps voluntarily) remained a commoner after
his wife was created a Viscountess.

inculcating Truth, Loyalty, Chastity, Courtesy, Liberality, Reverence for Women and Generosity to the Weak. But the real foundation of Privilege in Chivalric Times was practically Strength, Courage and Success among men, Beauty, Grace and Honour among women. These qualities being temporary, were not synonymous with Justice. The position of Divinity is an unstable one, depending on the attitude of the worshippers. When Chivalry faded out of men's hearts, women felt that the outer shell of custom meant little. It only set them on the shelf.

A tone of Chivalry affected the hearts of the traders and manufacturers of Chivalric Times, a tone healthier, because more founded on justice and equality. There was even then a confusion of ideas between return-value of labour abroad and labour at home; but there was no confusion about the return-values of similar labour performed by men or by women. Women were equal in all social guilds, and trading women were equal in trading guilds.

The notion that partnership in toil could justify the assumption of the whole proceeds of the common labours to the use and will of one of the partners did not dawn on the simpler minds of our ancestors. It took centuries of mistranslations of the first principles of government to let this partial idea develop into its modern complexity. In Prynne's "Fundamental Rights of English Freemen," p. 3, art. 7, we read, "That it is the ancient and undoubted right of every freeman that he hath a full and absolute propriety in his goods and estate. And that no taxes, taillages, loans, benevolences, or other charge ought to be commanded, imposed, or levied by the King or his Ministers, without common consent by Act of Parliament." In order that husbands might have the absolute proprietary right over the whole of the common property, it was gradually extinguished among wives; and the second right for them naturally lapsed in consequence of the other. The absorption of a married woman's property by her husband developed for her a massive code of legal restrictions, and a stern doctrine of civil disabilities. She was dissociated first from property, thence from privilege, finally she became property. This was but the natural outcome of the non-recognition of her Personal and Proprietary Rights. In any history, therefore, of British Freewomen, we must practically follow legal precedent, in assuming the non-existence of the *feme couverte*.

Through the different principles of inheritance, there have always been fewer heiresses than heirs; through the success of the various methods of protecting male professional and trade industries against female competition, there have always been fewer female owners of earned property; through the lower rate of women's wages, and various causes tending to disable single women even in the retention of property, these owners represented smaller incomes than did men of their own class.

Representative Freewomen, therefore, have always been

in a small minority. The dominance of a *temporary majority* sends a minority into the Opposition ; in which exile it lays plans for future action, when in the seesaw of political change its turn comes to rise again. The majority has always to consider the minority in its calculations and actions. But a *permanent majority*, consciously or unconsciously, labours to oust a *permanent minority* from recognised and recognisable existence even as an Opposition. By *always* being able to over-bear opinion, it makes the expression of opinion futile. Either it is concordant and unnecessary, or discordant and inoperative. The expression of either becomes a waste of time, and is soon denied. And thus women have been ousted by degrees from the building up of the superstructure of the English Constitution, in whose foundations they had been considered. The privilege of British Freewomen remained a recognised quantity for ages. Though that quantity became " small by degrees and beautifully less," it was not finally annihilated till the heart of the nineteenth century.

The process of diminution was hastened in periods of spasmodic activity through association of principles that should have worked in the opposite direction, had the principles been understood and applied in their purity. No doctrine is more antagonistic to the spirit and teaching of Christ than that of the subjection of women, and yet, though the change from the Druidic religion to the worship of Odin affected them but slightly, the changes within the Christian Creed mark epochs in their gradual enthralment; as, for instance, the sixteenth century Reformation and the seventeenth century Revival. On the suppression of the Monasteries, Abbots and Abbesses were alike extinguished. But the power and privilege of the Abbot in the House of Peers, as in the Church, survived in the Bishop. The extinction of the Abbess, without successor either in Church or State, took away finally the right of one class of representative women to sit in the Upper House. The suppression of the Social and Religious Guilds founded and supported by women in common with men, gave a seeming reason for later exclusion of Freewomen from trade guilds.

The loudest Puritan cry of the seventeenth century was, it is true, "No Bishop"; but the practical work Puritanism was really allowed to do in politics was to make the representation of women in the Lower House theoretically impossible.

As antagonistic to the doctrine of the subjection of women are the Principles of Liberty. How can men become truly free that ignore, for others, the liberties founded on the same reasonings by which they enfranchised themselves? Yet every great era in the Evolution of so-called *Popular Liberty* has been marked by contemporary restrictions of Feminine Freedom. Hence, in the seventeenth century, when hereditary serfdom was finally abolished, and when slavery, by purchase, became impossible in Britain, we first find the doctrine promulgated that tended to disfranchise women. When outbursts of fervid eloquence on "Liberty" were preparing the nation to lay out its millions in enfranchising even its colonial slaves, in 1832, the disfranchisement of women was effected by the use of a single statutory word, by the interpolation of "male" before "persons." When, on the 29th of June, 1867, William Lloyd Garrison, the champion of Negro Emancipation, was receiving an ovation at St. James's Hall, men were discussing in St. Stephen's whether to give women political existence or not. Though the single excluding word was erased from the Statute-book, the House and the Courts of Law next year determined that its spirit lingered there. When a new extension of the Suffrage took place in 1884, the claims of women were again disallowed. The new rights of men emphasised more strongly the old wrongs of women. A lowered qualification for the Franchise protected property, not only inherited or earned, but that which was only in the process of earning. This privilege of prospective property enormously increased the opportunities of earning. But *only* when its possession was vested in a man. Women's possession of property, more difficult to acquire through laws of Nature, custom, inheritance, marriage, and the protection of male industries, was further rendered less stable by their exclusion from the faintest voice in determining laws, taxation, and home and foreign policy. The progress of education has enriched public ideas, has altered the Content of public Conscience, has facilitated public discussion of facts and theories. The relations of representation to taxation are assailed. New bases of privilege are being proposed. There are those who hold that Property is no sound foundation on which to build a Constitution. Some would put in its place the notion of Justice, which others name the right of the Individual. But those who accept this are divided into two great classes, the first considering Justice in its own nature, and treating Individuals as the indivisible units to which Justice is to be applied, units not to be segregated by *any* test into groups receiving Justice or no Justice. The second class also considers Justice applicable to all individuals, but adds a rider that, in their opinion, *individuals can be only masculine.* Something in the construction of their minds permits them to harmonise, to their own satisfaction, two discordant ideas. Masculinity seems to them a natural basis of privilege—a solid foundation of Justice.

Others hold the older doctrines in a modified form, believing that individuality without qualification of individuals cannot provide a stable basis. If the idle and improvident, by mere force of numbers, are to dominate the industrious and the provident, the ends of justice would be defeated. By property or industry tests those are included who have interests to preserve. Those who help to support the State should have a voice in determining its action. No one is excluded from Enfranchisement thereby. A very moderate degree of industry or success will make it possible to anyone to attain the franchise. A worthy incentive to labour is a moral good. Amidst these thinkers there are also two classes : those who consider that the rights of women in themselves, and

in the property they inherit or acquire, are as important as
those of men, and should be made as stable ; and those
that, by combining two principles of Enfranchisement,
make a logical cross division, importing the totally unconnected dividing principle of sex into the consideration of
the rights of property.   What is simply *unjust*, when
individuals are selected on the basis of sex, becomes
both *illogical* and *unjust* when questions of sex are
imposed on those of property.   Sex is an inseparable
accident, and when accepted as the Basis of Justice,
closes the question ; property is a separable accident, and
must be considered upon different lines.   The various
objections to any simple, logical, homogeneous, and just
arrangement of the Bases of Privilege, while depending on
the doctrine of sex, are worked out by two sub-sections of
thinkers upon different lines.   One section says boldly,
" When persons qualified by property are also qualified by
masculinity, we grant them privilege."   The other section
analyses the attributes of masculinity, and applies each as
a separate test to the person qualified by property.   " The
physical force argument is the foundation of government,
most men are stronger than most women, therefore no
women must interfere in government," say they, in a
syllogism that all logicians must condemn.   Women
would "require an improved understanding to vote
for a member of Parliament." . . . "Women cannot
understand mathematics nor master the classics."
When women proved they could, the principle was
sent back further into statements that "their brains

were not heavy enough," "their moral force not strong enough." "Women have not written Shakespeare, composed Beethoven, painted Raphael, built St. Peter's." The understanding of proportional representation, and the far-reaching economic results of bi-metallism, have been seriously proposed as tests for women. But have the whole series, or *any one of them*, ever been applied to the mere male electors of the realm? When pressed hard on this point, these objectors, in their confusion, fall back upon precedent and on authority to prove that to be *legal* which they cannot prove to be *just or reasonable*. It is no conclusive argument in favour of anything that *it has been*, or else reformation would be impossible. But when the sole argument against its *being* is that it *has not been*, the consideration of Legality and of Precedent becomes a necessity to the advocates of Justice. Many mistakes have been taken for facts, many fallacious arguments based upon erroneous premises. A Review of the History of Women that have hitherto ever exercised any privilege is necessary for generalisations to be based thereon. For by this process we may unite the followers of Legality and Precedent with the worshippers of Justice and Equality, and the union of the two forces, like those of the sun and moon upon the sea, may raise the high "tide in the affairs of women that leads on to fortune."

The Review is encouraging in two aspects. In the light of the modern doctrine of Heredity, we see that our far-away ancestors held opinions to which we may hope that our successors may yet *revert;* and from Ancient History we find that a recognition of the existence of women in the State, far from being novel or revolutionary, would only be the fulfilling of the fundamental principles of the English Constitution.

CHAPTER III

"The country prospers when a woman rules."

IN order to simplify and classify the mass of material at hand, it is advisable to take by their degree the ranks of women among the Anglo-Normans. Among the Queens, only because they precede in order of time and of number, we may take first :

Queens Consort.—In Doomsday Book, Matilda, the wife of the Conqueror, is entered as holding of the King, many lands forfeited by the Saxons. "She was made the feudal possessor of the lands of Beortric, Earl of Gloucester, hence the practice of settling the Lordship of Bristol on the Queen generally prevailed for centuries. On her death in 1083, her lands went back to the King by feudal tenure. The Conqueror kept them in his own hands, meaning them for his and her youngest son Henry, who afterwards succeeded." (Seyer's "Memoirs of Bristol," chap. iv., p. 318.) Later queens had separate establishments, officers and privy purse. "The Aurum Reginæ, or Queen's Gold, is distinguished from all other debts and duties belonging to the Queen of this Realme.

All other revenues proceed to her from the grace of the King, this by the common law . . . which groweth upon all fines paid to the King, licenses, charters, pardons, of which she receives one-tenth part. After her death the King recovers his right to hold this tenth. This duty hath been enjoyed by the Queens from Eleanor, wife of Henry II., to Anne, second wife of Henry VIII." (Hakewell's speech in Parliament on Aurum Reginæ. Addit. MSS., Brit. Mus. 25, 255.)

Even to our own days Queens Consort have had the privilege of acting as *femes soles*. But in early times they exercised considerably more power in the State than we realise to-day. They sat in the Councils, even in the presence of the Kings, and gave their consent to measures along with Kings and Nobles. "The Queen-wife of England also superscribed her name *over* their warrants or letters of public direction or command, although in the time of Henry VIII. the fashion was that the Queens wrote their names over the left side of the first line of such warrants, and not *over* them as *the Kings do*" (Selden's "Titles of Honour"). But as many of the Queens Consort, though thus entitled to be ranked among "Freewomen," were not of native extraction, we do not dwell upon all their privileges, preferring to hasten on to those that indubitably were British Freewomen.

Queens Regnant.—The first critical moment in the History of Queens Regnant occurred at the death of Henry I., who had, as he considered, arranged satisfactorily for the succession of his daughter Matilda

His attempt proved that the French Salic Law had not been made law in England. A quaint account of his proceeding appears in the "Lives of the Berkeleys," published by the Gloucester Archæological Society, 1835, p. 2. "King Harri the first, third sonne of King William the Conqueror, had issue remaining one daughter named Maude . . . the sayd King Harri send for his foresayd daughter Maude the Emparice into England, and in open Parliament declared and ordeyned her to bee his eire. To whom there and then were sworen all the lordes of England, and made unto her sewte, admittinge her for his eire. Amongs whom principally and first was sworen Stephen, Earle of Boleyn, nevowe of the sayd King Harri the first." But as Selden says, "I do very well know that our perjured Barons, when they resolved to exclude Queen Maud from the English Throne, made this shameful pretence, 'that it would be a shame for so many nobles to be subject to one woman.' And yet you shall not read, that the Iceni, our Essex men, got any shame by that Boadicea, whom Gildas terms a lioness" (Janus Anglorum, chap. xii., p. 19). The same author, in noting the laws made by various kings, enters the reign of Stephen as that of an unrighteous king who had no time to make laws for the protection of the kingdom, because he had to fight in defence of his own unjust claim. "In 1136 Henry of England died, and Stephen, Earl of Boulogne, succeeded. At Mass on the Day of his Coronation, by some mistake, the peace of God was forgotten to be pronounced on the people " ("Antiquitates," Camden). Prynne calls him "the perjured usurping King Stephen." The general uncertainty of the succession is betokened in the struggle. Very probably had there not been a Stephen to stir up the nobles, the country might have rested peaceably under the rule of Matilda.

It seems strange that the oldest Charters of the express creation of the title of Comes (Count or Earl) are those of Queen Maud, who first created the Earldom of Essex and the Earldom of Hereford. To Aubrey de Vere also she granted the Earldom of Cambridge, or another title if he preferred it, and he chose the Earldom of Oxford. A struggle like the Wars of the Roses was closed by the death of Stephen and the peaceable succession of Matilda's son, Henry II.

Another lady of the family was supplanted by the proverbially "cruel uncle." King John in 1202 made prisoners of his nephew, Arthur, Duke of Brittany, and the Princess Eleanor, his sister, called "The Beauty of Brittany." Arthur is supposed to have been murdered by his uncle, and Eleanor was confined for forty years in Bristol Castle. A true daughter of Constance of Brittany, the wife of Geoffrey, she is said to have possessed a high and invincible spirit, and to have constantly insisted on her right to the throne, which was probably the reason that she spent her life in captivity. (*See* the Close Rolls of the Tower of London, and the Introduction xxxv.)

The second real crisis was that which closed the

Wars of the Roses. Another Stephen appeared in Henry VII., who, fortunately for the people, simplified matters by marrying Elizabeth of York, the rightful heir. Jealous in the extreme of his wife's prerogative, he used his high hand as the conqueror of Richard III. and the kingdom, delayed her coronation as long as he dared, ignored her in his councils, and magnified his relation as husband, to the extinction of her glory as Queen.

Henry VIII. enjoyed to the full the advantage of an undisputed succession. He restricted the rights of Queens Consort, as his father had ignored the rights of Queens Regnant. A strange Nemesis followed, foretold in the so-called prophecies of Merlin. That these really were talked of, before the events occurred, can be proved by MSS. among the uncalendared papers, temp. Henry VIII., Public Record Office. There is in full "the Examination of John Ryan of St. Botolphs, Fruiterer, concerning discourses which he heard at the Bell on Tower Hill, Prophecies of Merlin, that there never again would be King crowned of England after the King's son Prince Edward, 22nd August, 1538." James V. of Scotland had sadly said on his death-bed, "The kingdom came with a lass, and it will go with a lass." So it was to be in England. The pale, sickly youth who succeeded, third of the Tudors, died without wife or child, and on the steps of the throne stood four Royal women, whose lives form the most interesting period of national history. Each of them had a special claim. Mary, pronounced illegitimate by the Protestant party, and by statute of Parliament, inherited through her father's *will* alone ; Elizabeth, pronounced illegitimate by the Catholic party, and by a similar statute, stood second in that will ; Mary, Queen of Scotland and of France, showed flawless descent from Margaret, the elder sister of Henry VIII. ; and Lady Jane Grey could prove like flawless descent from Mary, Henry's younger sister.

Henry, a despot even " by his dead hand," had, failing Edward, his daughters, Mary and Elizabeth, left the crown to the heirs of his sister Mary. These were her daughters Frances, married to Henry Grey, Duke of Suffolk, and Ellinor, married to the Earl of Cumberland.

Edward VI., not a minor by the laws of England, that allowed Government to commence at fourteen years, considered both his sisters illegitimate under his father's statutes, preferring of the two Elizabeth's claim. But for the peace of the kingdom, as he thought, he left by *will* the crown to Lady Jane Grey, the eldest daughter of Frances, Duchess of Suffolk (still alive), ignoring, as his father had done, the prior claims of Mary, Queen of Scotland and of France. The results of the complication are too well known to be here rehearsed.

The first act of Mary Tudor was to establish her own legitimacy, the honour of her mother, and the power of the Pope ; her second was to establish the office of Queen Regnant " by Statute to be so clear that none but the malitious and ignorant could be induced and persuaded unto this Error and Folly to think that her Highness

coulde ne should have enjoye and use such like Royal
Authoritie . . nor doo ne execute and use all things
concerning the Statutes (in which only the name of the
King was expressed) as the Kinges of this Realme, her
most noble Progenitours have heretofore doon, used and
exercised " (1 Mar. I., Sessio Tertia, c. i., 1553-4).

Both she and her sister, at their coronations, were
girt with the sword of State, and invested with the
spurs of knighthood, to show that they were military
as well as civil rulers. Fortunately for her country
and for herself, Elizabeth lived and died a maiden
Queen. The bitter consequences of her sister's Spanish
alliance taught her the importance of independence
as a ruler. Whatever we may individually think of
her character, all must allow her reign to have been in
every way the most brilliant in the history of our country, only equalled in our own times by that of a Matron
Queen, who has held the reins of government in her own
hand and whose husband lived in the land but as Prince
Consort. (*See* Sir Theodore Martin's "Life of The Prince
Consort.") Queen Anne's reign is also worthy of note,
and can bear comparison with that of most Kings, for
its military successes and its literary activities.

Queens Regent.—Selden * argues against Bodin of
Anjou, who upheld the Salic Law, "are not discretion
and strength, courage and the arts of government, more
to be desired and required in those who have the tuition
of kings in their minority, than in the kings themselves

* "Janus Anglorum," chap. xii., p. 19.

till they are come of age?" He considers the French use of Queens as Regents to be destructive of their own theories.

Queens as Regent-Tutors of young kings have not held the same position in England as they did in France or in Scotland. But as governing Regents and Viceroys they have often done good service.* William of Normandy more than once left the country in charge of his Queen. Richard I., by commission, appointed his mother Eleanor to be Regent of the kingdom in his absence, and wrote to her to find the money for his ransom when imprisoned abroad. She sat as Judge in the Curia Regis, taking her seat on the King's Bench by right of her office. She granted concessions to the inhabitants of Oléron (to women as to men) even down to the reign of John (1 John; *see* "Rymer's Fœdera"). Edward III. found his Queen Philippa a Queen Regent worthy of himself. Henry V. appointed his mother as Regent in his absence, and even Henry VIII., when he went abroad on his last French war, left his Queen, Catherine Parr, Governor of the kingdom. I have gone through their correspondence in the Public Record Office, and it bears ample testimony to her capability and his trust in her judgment. In "Olive *versus* Ingram," 1739, it is noted, "Queen Caroline was once appointed Regentor

---

* "The Witenagemot decided that Aelfgyfu, Hurthacnute's mother, should dwell at Winchester, with the King her son's Huscarls, and hold all Wessex under his authority." (*Anglo-Saxon Chronicle*, f. 130, 1036.)

of the Kingdom." (7 Modern Reports, pp. 263, 276.) . . .

It was with little less than Viceregal splendour and power that Joan, Dowager Countess of Pembroke, ruled the Palatinate for nine years in the reign of Edward I., or Isabel de Burgo in that of Edward II., or Agnes de Hastings in that of Edward III.; ruling in the stead of their sons until the youths attained majority at the age of twenty-one.

Princess Beatrice, youngest child of Queen Victoria, was made Governor of the Isle of Wight by her mother.

CHAPTER IV

"Noblesse Oblige."

In Selden's "Titles of Honour," iii., 890, he says: "Of feminine titles some are immediately created in women, some are communicated by their husbands, others are transmitted to them from their ancestors, and some also are given them as consequents only of the dignity of their husbands and parents." Of "immediate creation" he gives the example of Margaret, Countess of Norfolk, created by Richard II. Duchess of Norfolk, wherein the investiture is mentioned by the patent to be by putting on her the cap of honour "recompensatio meritorum." Through lapsed inheritance, Margaret Plantagenet, widow of Sir Richard Pole, was made Countess of Salisbury in her own right by Henry VIII., 1513. (*See* Froude's "History of England," II., 66-67.) Henry VIII. also created Anne Boleyn Marchioness of Pembroke. James I. created Lady Mary Compton the Countess of Buckingham in her husband's lifetime, without permitting him to share the honour. (*See* "Marshall's Genealogist," N.S., lv., 65.) He also created Lady

40

Finch first Viscountess of Maidstone, and afterwards Countess of Winchilsea, limiting inheritance to heirs of her body.

Anne Bayning, wife of James Murray, was created Viscountess Bayning of Foxley in 1674. Several titles have been granted for discreditable causes, too few for "recompensatio meritorum." Men that were merely rich have been made peers. Women that have been truly noble have not been made noble by Letters Patent. Yet we have a few examples. Fraulein Lehzen (Queen Victoria's governess) was made a Baroness by George IV. in recognition of her services. (*See* "Personal Life of Queen Victoria," by Mrs. Tooley, p. 51.)

"There was once a female Baronet, Dame Maria Bolles of Osberton, Nottinghamshire" (Collections and Recollections, G. W. Erskine Russell, p. 265). The Baroness Burdett - Coutts was ennobled by Queen Victoria for her philanthropy.

In 1868 Mrs. D'Israeli was raised to the Peerage as Viscountess Beaconsfield in her husband's lifetime, he remaining a commoner. Mr. D'Israeli was not made a Peer until after her death.

In 1891 Emily Smith, the widow of the Right Hon. William Henry Smith, was raised to the Peerage by the title of Viscountess Hambledon. Susan Agnes Macdonald was created Baroness Macdonald of Earnscliffe.

The titles that women received from their husbands were doubtless intended more as an honour to their husbands than to themselves, though they carried, at times, considerable privileges along with them. They bore them as widows until their death, sometimes with the full honours and powers their husbands had borne. They frequently bore their first husband's title after another marriage, as did the Countess of Southampton, who remained officially so, after her second marriage to Sir Thomas Heneage, and her third to Sir William Harvey.

There are some curious cases of titles being *assigned.* Ranulph, Earl of Chester and Lincoln, granted the Earldom of Lincoln to his sister, the Lady Hawise de Quency. She afterwards granted the title to John de Lacy, who had married her daughter Margaret, a grant confirmed by the King in a charter, limiting the inheritance to the heirs of Margaret.

I have already noted the two limitations of a daughter's inheritance of property. The same affected titles. But having inherited, she became endowed with every privilege to the full; and every duty was exacted of her to the utmost.

Women paid Homage.—In spite of many careless remarks to the contrary, women paid homage. "John, heir of the Devereux, died under age; his sister Joane, making proof of her age, and doing her homage, had Livery of the Lands of her Inheritance" (2 Ric. II., Dugdale, 117). (*See* Littleton upon Tenures, Form of Homage, 87, 88.)

The summons to Ladies as well as to Lords for aids to the King was "de fide et homagio."

It is true that at some periods widows did not pay homage for the lands of their deceased husbands ; but neither then did men pay homage for the lands of their deceased wives, holding only by " the Courtesy of England." " Because if homage be given, it might never return to the lawful heir " ("Statutes of the Realm, Lands held by Courtesy," vol. i., p. 220).

Received Homage.—"Homage may be done to any free person, whether male or female, whether of full age or otherwise, whether Clergy or Lay." (Glanville, B. IX., c. iii. Coke upon Littleton, 67ᵃ). Many examples are given in the "Rotuli Hundredorum," "Testa de Nevil," and "Kirkby's Inquest." Isabella and Idonea de Veteripont insisted on Fealty and Homage from the inhabitants of Appleby (4 Edward I.), as did Anne Clifford later (Nicolson's " History of Westmoreland," v. 2). One curious distinction comes in here between the sexes, as a result of the system of *co-parceny* among sisters. A brother might pay homage to his brother, the heir by primogeniture, but not a sister to her sister,* because they were equal. The statute of 20 Henry III. (1235) enacted that " the law regarding sisters, co-heirs, be used for Ireland as in England, that the eldest sister only pay Homage to the Overlord or to the King in her own name and that of her sisters, but that the sisters do

* In Kent, brothers did not pay homage to each other, but if a brother or a sister granted his or her land to be held by a brother or a sister, then homage might be paid for it before the Statute *Quia Emptores*, 18 Edward I.

not pay Homage to the sister, for that would be to make her Seigneuress over the other sisters" (Rot. Parl., 20 Henry III.).

They could hold Courts Baron.—A petition, 16 Richard II., appears, praying that no Liegeman should be *compelled* to appear at the Courts and Councils of the Lord or of the Lady to reply for his freehold. "In 4 Edward I., Ida Botetourt held a Court at Chykenhalle, Trenchfoil, as did John Botetourt, the 20th year of the same King." (Morant's Essex, vol. ii., p. 81.)

In the Rotuli Hundredorum, Edward I., many women are entered as holding Courts of Frank-pledge and Assizes of Bread and Ale, and as having a Gallows in their Jurisdiction, as "Johanna de Huntingfeud held view of Frank-pledge in the Hundred of Poppeworth, Canterbury," vol. i., p. 53. Elena de la Zouche, also Agnes de Vescy, and Elena de Valtibus in Dorsetshire, the Countess of Leycester at Essedon in Buckinghamshire. ("Relation of Women to the State in past times." Helen Blackburn, *National Review*, Nov., 1886.) Margaret, Countess of Derby, held the town of Yoxhall in Dower, and "held plea in her Court of all things usual, except of forbidden distress, and had view of Frank-pledge, without the cognizance of the Sheriff as the Earl held them." (*See* Shaw's Staffordshire, Yoxhall.)

The Countess Lucy kept her Courts at Spalding during the banishment of her first husband, Yvo de Taillebois. (Selby's "Genealogist," 1889, p. 70.) The Pipe Roll of 31 Hen. I. shows that she had agreed to pay the King

100 marks for the privilege of administering justice among her tenants (homines) (*See* p. 64.)

In Anne Clifford's Diary, Harl. MS., 6177, appears :

" 1650. This time of my staying in Westmoreland I employed myself in building and reparation at Skipton and Barden Towers, and in causing ye bounds to be ridden and my Courts kept in my sundry mannors in Craven . . . ."

" 1653. In the beginning of this year did I cause several Courts to be kept in my name in divers of my mannors in this Country."

" 1659. And ye Aprill after, did I cause my old decayed Castle of Brough to be repaired, and also the Tower called the Roman Tower in ye said Castle, and a Court-House for keeping of my Courts."

There is preserved in Swansea a charter granted, 2 Edward III., to Aliva, wife of John de Mowbray, of the land of Gower. It recites and confirms various previous charters of the land of Gower, with the appurtenances, and *all manner of Jurisdictions*, and all Royal Liberties and free customs which Gilbert de Clare, the son of Richard de Clare, theretofore Earl of Gloucester and Hertford, had in his land of Glamorgan. (Report of Municipal Corporations, 1835, p. 383.)

This practice seems to have long survived in modified forms. In the same Report, p. 2850, regarding the Borough of Ruthin : " It was in evidence, and was indeed frankly admitted by the deputy-steward, that upon impanelling the jury at the Borough Court Leet, it is the

uniform practice for some agent of the Lady of the Manor
to address a letter, which is delivered to the foreman of
the jury in their retiring-room, recommending two persons
as aldermen, who are invariably elected. As a part of
this system, it was proved that in many instances the
duties and fees payable on the admission of burgesses to
their freedom had been defrayed by the Lady of the
Manor; and that the uncontrolled power of impanelling
the jury was left to her agent. The only answer furnished
by the deputy-steward was that he had taken for his
guide the usage of the place, as pursued by his predecessors, without reference to charters, which had only of
late years come under discussion." Also in page 2840,
regarding Rhuddlan : "As far as any ruling body or
corporation can be said to subsist in a borough thus
circumstanced, the Lady of the Manor must be considered to elect that body ; for the Steward of the Court
Leet is appointed by her during pleasure ; and he gives
the constables a list of the persons who are to serve on
the jury by whom the two bailiffs, the only subsisting
officers of the corporation, are chosen." The Lady of
the Manor there also paid the constables.

Held by Military Service.—There were 15 ladies
summoned for military service against Wales " de fide et
homagio," in 5 Edward I., and again in 10 Edward I.
Among these were Devorgilla de Balliol, Agnes de Vescy,
Dionysia de Monte Canisio, and Margaret de Ros. A
writ was issued to Isabella de Ros, commanding her " de
fide et homagio " to send her service to the muster at

Portsmouth for the King's expedition to Gascony, 14th
June, 1234. Elena de Lucy was summoned from the
county of Northampton "to perform military service in
parts beyond the sea. Muster at London, 7th July, 25
Edward I." Joan Disney of Lincoln was summoned "to
perform military service against the Scots. Muster at
London, 7th July, 25 Edward I." These are but a few
selected from many others that appear in Palgrave's
Parliamentary Writs. It is true that a substitute might
be sent by anyone, *male or female*, with reasonable excuse.
"On 16th April, 1303, proclamation was made that all
prelates, persons of religion, women and persons who
were unfit for military service, who were willing to com-
mute their service by fines, might appear before the
Barons of the Exchequer at York on 17th May ensuing.
Otherwise they, or their substitutes, must appear at the
muster at Berwick on the 26th May." "A writ of
Distringas was issued against Juliana de Averenches for
not coming to serve in the King's army, and for not
making fine, upon summons ad habendum Servicium."
(Brevia Retornabilia, Mich. 34 Edward I. Rot. 81 a.)
"In 10 Edward III., Isabel, the eldest of the daughters
and heiresses of Bartholomew Davyllers, paid a fine to
the King of 40s., as relief for her share of the
Manor of Brone in Suffolk, which is held of the King in
Capite (by grand Serjeanty) by the service of leading all
the foot-soldiers of Norfolk and Suffolk into the war
against Wales, taking 4d. for each man for his expenses,
for 40 days, and after that, Bartholomew and his men to

remain at the King's charges. For her fourth share, the said Isabel made Homage to the King, in the fifth year of his reign." (Madox, Baronia Anglica, 239 *et seq.*)

Palgrave's Parliamentary Writs give long lists of women holding castles, towns, and military feods in 9 Edward II., and Harl. MS., 4219, in "Hundreda, Civitates, Burgi, et Villæ in Comitatu Norfolk et *Domini* eorundem," gives many names of women. "Abbatissa de Shaftesbury owes service of three military feuds. . . . Abbatissa de Wilton owes service of two military feuds." "Lady Juliana de Leybourne (Kent) owes service of two military feuds." (Madox, Baronia Anglica.)

Margaret, widow of Lord Edmund Mortimer, was charged with providing one hundred men for the wars in Scotland out of her lands at Key and Warthenon. (Dugdale's "Peerage and Baronetage," vol. i., p. 173.)

In 3 Edward II. writs docketed "De summonicione servicii Regis" were issued to Abbots and Abbesses alike for military aid against the Scots, "de fide et dilectione"; and to Nobles, Lords and Ladies alike "in fide et homagio." On the 13th September following Domina Maria de Graham proffers the service of two knights' fees for all her lands in England, performed by four servants with four barded horses; and many noble ladies offer equivalent service.

Joane Plantagenet, the Fair Maid of Kent, inherited from her brother the Earldom of Kent, and from her mother the Barony of Wake, by which she was styled the Lady of Wake. She married Sir Thomas de Holland, who, through her, became Earl of Kent without creation. Her son Thomas succeeded both. His widow Alicia died possessed of 27 manors held by direct feudal or military tenure, beside many freeholds. (*See* " Inquisitions *Post-Mortem* " ; 4 Henry IV.)

They could be Knights.—Not only in Romances, not only in Spenser's " Faery Queene," but in books of Chivalry, we may see that women could be knights. Mary and Elizabeth were made knights before they were made Queens. When Queen Elizabeth took upon herself the command of her forces at the threatened Spanish Invasion, she knighted Mary, wife of Sir Hugh Cholmondeley, for her valiant address. She was ever after called The Bold Lady of Cheshire. (*See* Miss Strickland's " Lives of Queens of England—Elizabeth," p. 571. Also Nichol's "Progresses of King James I.," vol. iii., p. 436.*)

Abergavenny Castle was held by knight's service. William, Baron Cantilupe, by marrying Eva, daughter and co-heir of William, Lord Braose, obtained the Castle and Lands. Her tomb in St. Mary's Church, Abergavenny, 1246, is of interest as being the earliest

---

* The Begum of Bhopal was made a Lady Knight, of the most noble order of Queen Victoria, on the proclamation of the Queen as Empress of India, 1st January, 1877. In 1879, when Queen Victoria became a great-grandmother, she invested twelve noble Ladies of her Court with the Imperial Order of the Crown of India. (*See* the " Personal Life of Queen Victoria," Mrs. Sarah Tooley, p. 222.)

stone effigy of a woman known in England. Her daughter, Eva de Cantilupe, succeeded to the barony and the castle, and was a knight. Her tomb is the only instance known of the stone effigy of a woman adorned with the insignia of knighthood, 1247. In 1589 Edward Neville sued for the Barony as being entailed in the Heir Male. His suit was at first refused. The Lord Chief-Justice Popham determined "that there was no right at all in the Heir Male; the common Custom of England doth wholly favour the Heir General . . . and Her Majesty would require to make a new creation to prefer the Heir Male to the Heir Female" (Sir Harris Nicolas' "Historic Peerages," p. 15). But appeal followed appeal against Sir Thomas Fane and his wife Mary, only daughter and heir of Henry, Lord and Baron of Burgavenny, who had died 8th February, 29 Elizabeth, 1586. They pleaded that Richard Neville, Baron Burgavenny and Earl of Westmoreland, had died, 9 Henry V., leaving an only child, Elizabeth, who married Sir Edward Neville, and "he was called Baron Burgavenny in right of his wife, according to the ancient and approved custom of this realme from all antiquity in like cases." (Harl. MS. 6778, p. 7.) "The Pedigree of the Barony of Burgavenny from Eva, wife to William Cantilupe, Lady Proprietary of Burgavenny. The book of Mr. Somerset Herald, proving the title to be in Dame Mary Fane." (State Papers—Dom. Ser. Eliz. CCXIX., 7th December, 1588.) "Why should not a woman be a Baroness, as a Countess-Marshal, to be the King's

Champion, or to hold her lands by Knight's Service?"
Many examples of women doing so are brought forward.
"The Commonwealth would suffer by the stopping of
Baronies held by and through women . . . the common
law and the law of chivalry do hold women capable of
such dignities . . . our fathers considered daughters not
less children than sons . . . heirs to tenures by martial
service . . . with privilege and liberty of deputation."
(Harl. MS., *see* above.) The suit hung on long; finally
the House of Lords decided on 25th May, 2 James I.,
against all precedent, that the Barony should descend to
the Heir Male, Edward Neville. Lady Fane was, however, granted another Barony formerly owned by her
family, the Barony of Despencer. Lady Mary Fane,
Baroness Despencer, died 25th May, 1604, and was
succeeded by her son, Francis, who was also created
Baron Burgersh and Earl of Westmoreland. (*See*
"Burke's Peerage.") It is difficult to understand how
this decision could be arrived at, in spite of precedent
and of Common Law. It marks the beginning of the
change of view in regard to women, which developed
during the seventeenth century. Margaret, wife of
Sampson Lemark, had claimed the Barony of Dacres,
as sister and heir to Gregory, late Lord Dacres, and
her claim was allowed by Lord Burleigh, 28th February,
24 Eliz., 1582-3.

**Inherited Public Office associated with the Title or
Property.**—The story of Ela of Salisbury illustrates the
views with which the early Normans regarded heiresses.

She was born in 1188. Her father, the Earl of Salisbury, died 1196, leaving her sole heir. She inherited both title and lands before his three brothers. Her mother conveyed her away secretly to a castle in Normandy, to save her from possible dangers during her minority. An English knight, William Talbot, romantically undertook, as a troubadour, to discover her whereabouts, and, after two years, brought her back to England. King Richard betrothed her as a Royal ward to his half-brother, William Longepée, son of Fair Rosamund, who became, through her, Earl of Salisbury. At King John's coronation at Westminster, William, Earl of Salisbury, is noted as being present among the throng of nobility. (*See* "Roger Hoveden.") He died 1226, leaving four sons and four daughters. Though besieged with suitors, Ela preferred a "free widowhood" to selecting another Earl Salisbury. When her son came of age he claimed investiture of the Earldom, but the King refused it *judicialiter*, by the advice of the Judges, and according to the dictates of Law. The Earldom and the government of the Castle of Sarum were vested in Ela, not in her dead husband.

The office of Sheriff of Wiltshire, her right by inheritance, she exercised in person until 21 Hen. III., when, probably to facilitate her son's entrance into the Earldom, she retired as Abbess to the Abbey of Lacock, founded by herself.* Even then, however, the youth did not

---

* "12 Henry III., Sheriff of Wiltshire, Eliza. Comitissa Saresb. dep. John Dacres.
"16 Henry III., Eliza, Comitissa Saresb. dep. John Dacres.

receive the title, and she survived both son and grandson. The note to this biography adds : " Though the law of female descent, as applied to baronies by writ, has long ceased to govern the descent of earldoms, it certainly did during the first centuries after the Norman Conquest." (Bowle's " History of Lacock Abbey.") Nicholaa de Camville was Sheriff of Lincoln, in the time of John. " The Countess Dowager of Cornwall is Sheriff of Rutland, deputy Gilbert Holm." (*See* Maitland's " Records of Parliament," 35 Edward I., 1305.)

Isabella and Idonea de Veteripont, who afterwards married Roger de Clifford, and Roger de Leybourn jointly held the office of **High Sheriff of Westmoreland,** and insisted on the Burghers bringing their cases to them personally, 15 Ed. I. The office was held afterwards, also in person, during the reigns of the Stuarts, by the brave Anne de Clifford, Countess of Dorset, Pembroke, and Montgomery, and Baroness of Westmoreland. In virtue of her office, she sat on the Bench of Justices in the Court of Assizes at Appleby. (Durnford and East's " Term Reports," vol. ii., p. 397, Rex *v.* Stubbs ; Butler's Note to Coke upon Littleton, 326ª. Nicolson's " History of Westmoreland," vol. ii., p. 20.) " As

---

" 20 Henry III., Eliza. Comitissa Saresb. dep. Robert de Hagen. " 21 Henry III., Eliza. Comitissa Saresb. . . ."

(*See* Fuller's Worthies, Wiltshire.)

" In this Abbey is still preserved Henry III.'s Magna Charta of 1225, sent to Ela, Countess of Salisbury, who at that time held the Shrievalty of the County of Wilts."

(*National Gazetteer*, S. N. Laycock.)

the King came out of Scotland, when he lay at York, there was a striffe between my father and my Lord Burleigh, who was then President, who should carie the sword; but it was adjudged to my father's side, because it was his Office by Inheritance, and so it is lineally descended on me" (Anne Clifford's Diary, Harl. MS., 6177). We may add here, though belonging properly to the following chapter, a parallel case:

" William Balderstone had two co-heiresses, Isabel and Jane. Isabel married Sir Robert Harrington of Hornby, and Jane, first Sir Ralph Langton, and second Sir John Pilkington. When Jane was " the young widow" of Sir Ralph Langton, in 1462, she, along with her sister Isabella and Sir Robert Harrington, her sister's husband, appeared in Court to vindicate their right to the offices of the **Baylywicks of the Wapentakes** of Amoundernes and Blakeburnshire, peacefully occupied by their ancestors time out of mind, and claimed by one Giles Beeston, on the plea of Letters Patent. Giles not appearing, judgment was given in their favour, and a preceipt issued accordingly to the Sheriff at the Castle of Leicester, 28th May, 2 Ed. IV. (Townley MSS.; Whittaker's " History of Whalley," vol. ii., p. 358, 4th edition, 1876).

The word Bailiwick was then applied to the office of a Sheriff, and to the district under him. " Every Sheriff of England shall reside within his Bailiwick." (*See* 4 Henry IV., c. v.; " Statutes of the Realm," vol. ii.)

" Guy de Beauchamp, late Earl of Warwick, held the

manor of Southanton as of inheritance from his deceased wife Alicia, by the Sergeanty of bearing a rod before the Justices in Eyre in the county." (9 Edward II., Blount's Tenures.)

Marshal.—Isabel de Clare, only daughter of Richard de Clare, Earl of Pembroke, brought the Earldom into the family of the Marshals of England by marrying William le Marshal. She had five sons (each of whom succeeded to the Office without leaving an heir of his body) and five daughters. The eldest of these, Maud, Countess of Norfolk, received as her share of the family property the Castles of Strigail and Cuniberg, and, with them, the office of Marshal, and in the 30 Hen. III. "received Livery by the King himself of the Marshal's Rod, being the eldest who by inheritance ought to enjoy that great office by descent from Walter Marischal sometime the Earl of Pembroke. Whereupon the Lord Treasurer and the Barons of the Exchequer had command to cause her to have all rights thereto belonging and to admit of such a deputy to sit in the Exchequer for her as she should assign." (Dugdale's Peerage, vol. i., p. 77.) Her son Roger exercised it during the remainder of her life and succeeded her.

Alicia de Bigod, his widow, succeeded him in his honour. I find among the petitions to the Council of 35 Edward I., held in Carlisle, one of "Alicia de Bygod Comitissa Mareschall" to be allowed to send a proxy to the Parliament of the King, "posuit loco suo, Johem Bluet militem, vel Johem de Fremlingham ad sequend

. . . pro dote sua coram Rege et consilio suo." This must have been granted ; both of these proxies appear in her name in the Parliament Roll of 35 Edward I. But she was summoned by writ personally *(*22nd January), in right of her office, to meet Edward II. and his bride at Dover on or about 4th February. (1 Edward II. ; Palgrave's " Parliamentary Writs.")

The office of Marshal and title of Earl of Norfolk were afterwards given " in tail general " to Thomas Brother-ton, son of Edward I. and brother of Edward II. His daughter Margaret inherited the office with the title and arms, as she appears as " Margaret, Countess-Marshal " in the Parliament Roll of 1 Richard II.* (Rot. Parl., 713.)

In the petition of John, Earl Marshal, for precedence over Earl Warwick, he says that " Thomas of Brotherton was son of Edward I., and bore the Royal arms. Of him came Margaret, of whom came Elizabeth, of whom came Thomas, of whom came John, now Erle Marechal, and so apperteneth ye said place in yis Riall court to this Lord Earl Mareshal by cause of the blode and armes Riall with ye said possession " (Rot. Parl., 3 Henry VI.) The office afterwards fell to the Mowbrays. Anne Mowbray, heiress, married the young Duke of York, second son

---

* " Henry le Piercy, Lord Piercy, was by writ authorised to exercise the place of Marshal of England *for that time*, saving to everyone their right, for that the claim which Margaret, daughter and heir to Thomas of Brotherton, late Earl of Norfolk, and Marshal of England, laid thereto could not so sodenly be discussed." (Harl. MS., 980, f. 14.)

of Edward IV., at the age of four years. She carried the office of Marshal to him, but he died in the Tower with his brother, Edward V., and his uncle seized the title.

"Adeline de Broc held possession of her Guildford estates by the service of being **Marshal in the King's Court**." (Blount's Tenures, Temp. Henry II.) "It was adjudged in Banco Regis, Car. I., that the Office of Marshal of that Court well descended to a *feme*, and that she might exercise it by deputy if she pleased." (B. R. Callis on Sewers, 250.) "The petition of Rose, The Marshall, against the Abbot of Westminster for Trespass" (Maitland's "Records of Parliament," 33 Edward I., 1305), was probably the more limited office of the Court.

High Constable.—Humphrey de Bohun, Earl of Hereford and Essex, held the manors of Harlefield, Newnam, and Whytenhurst, County Gloucester, by the service of High Constable. He left two daughters, but the elder, Eleanor, succeeded to the office, which she conveyed to her husband, Thomas of Woodstock, who exercised it for her; the younger sister, Mary, marrying Henry Plantagenet of Bolingbroke, afterwards Henry IV.*

* "Humfrey de Bohune, Earl of Hereford, was by tenure Constable of England (which is a judge in martial affairs), and he died without issue male, by reason whereof the office (among other things) descended to his two daughters and co-heirs; and in 11 Eliz. (Dyer. 285, B. 39), it is holden for law that although this was an office or justice, yet they might execute the same by deputy; for in truth women were unfit martialists to judge of matters of that nature; and yet it is clear a deputy doth nothing in his own name, but in the name of his master or mistress, therefore the Martial Court was

High Steward.—Henry, Earl of Leicester, through the Barony of Hinckley held the office of High Steward of England. He died, leaving two daughters, the elder of whom, having married abroad, left the dignity free to her sister, who married John of Gaunt, fourth son of Edward III. Through her right he exercised the office of Steward, which their son, Henry IV., carried back to the Crown.

High Chamberlain.—Justice Ashurst, from the King's Bench in 1788, notes that women have served the office of High Chamberlain (Rex *v.* Stubbs. 2 Term Reports, Durnford *v.* Easts, p. 395.) I have not yet found the name of the lady to whom he refers. " Richard Neville, Earl of Warwick, was one of the Chamberlains of the Exchequer, in right of Anne, his late wife, sister and heir of Henry, late Duke of Warwick, Chamberlain of Exchequer." (Issue Roll. Mich. 23rd February, 32 Henry VI.) (*See* also " Officers of the King, Deputy Chamberlain of the Exchequer.") The note says : "Of the two hereditary Chamberlainships one seems to have been vested in the Earl of Warwick, while the other,

to be kept in their names . . . and doth not our law temporal and spiritual admit of women to be executrixes and administratrixes? And hereby they have the ruling or ordering of great estates ; and many times they are guardianesses in chivalry, and have thereby also the government of many great heirs in the kingdom and of their estates." (*See* Callis on Sewers, p. 251 : quoted in the " Encyclopædia of the Laws of England," xii., 715, 716. Callis refers also to the Duke of Buckingham's cases, in which all the Judges of England decided it to be clear law. *See* also S. C. Keilway, 170[b], 4 Inst. 127, Coke upon Littleton, 165[a].)

which had belonged to Isabella, Countess of Albe-marle, seems to have been in the King's hand. ("Maitland and Madox," vol. ii., p. 30.) "Catherine, sole daughter and heir to the last Lord Willoughby d'Eresby, became fourth wife to Charles Brandon, Duke of Suffolk. She afterwards married Thomas Bertie, and her son was Peregrine, Lord Willoughby d'Eresby, who married Mary, daughter of the Earl of Oxford, whose son Robert (1 Jac. I.) inherited the title and Office of High Chamberlain." (Dugdale. Hargrave's Note 8 in Coke upon Littleton, 165ᵃ. *See* Collin's Peerage). We all know that the Baroness Willoughby d'Eresby held the Office down to our own times, though she allowed her son to exercise it as her deputy.

"The Manor of Hornmede, Hertforde, the Lady Lora de Saundford holds as a Serjeanty of our Lord the King by being Chamberlain to our Lady the Queen." (7 Edward I., Rot., 39.) (Blount's Tenures, p. 60.)

Ela, third daughter of Ela of Salisbury, foundress of Lacock, in 1285 was returned as holding the Manor of Hoke-Norton in Oxfordshire *in capite* by the Serjeanty of carving before our Lord the King on Christmas Day, when she had for her fee the King's knife with which she cut. (Placit. Coron., 14 Edward I., Rot., 30. Bowle's "History of Lacock Abbey," p. 160, ed. 1679; p. 166, 1874.) Anne, who was the wife of Sir John Hastings, Earl of Pembroke, who held the manor of Ashley in Norfolk of the King by Grant Serjeanty, viz., to perform the Office of the Napery at his coronation, was adjudged to make a deputy, because a woman cannot do it in person, and thereupon she deputed Sir Thomas Blount. (Coke upon Littleton, 107ᵇ.)

Champion.—The Manor of Scrivelby was held by the Dymocks on condition of the possessor acting as King's Champion.* When the heiress, Margaret, inherited the property, she inherited the Office, which her son, Thomas Dymock, performed for her at the coronation of Henry IV.

"The office of Champion at the last coronation was in a woman, who applied in that case to make a deputy." (7 Mod. Rep., p. 263, "Olive *versus* Ingram," 1739. Co. Litt., 108.)

In the "History of Scotland" we find a notable case of a woman being a *King-maker.* The only available representative of the ancient family who had the hereditary right, Isabella, Countess of Buchan, crowned King Robert the Bruce. When Edward I. next overran Scotland he seized her and imprisoned her for her courage and loyalty in a wooden cage on the ramparts of Berwick Castle.

They could be Governors of Royal Castles.—Isabella de Fortibus held the Borough and Camp of Plympton, and governed the Isle of Wight. In 8 and 9 Edward II. there was a settlement of Hugo de Courtenay's petition to succeed to his kinswoman, Isabella de Fortibus, in governance of the Isle of Wight, etc. Isabella de Vesci

* " The Dymocks derived the Championship through the marriage of Sir John Dymock to Margaret de Ludlow, daughter of Joane de Marmyon and Sir Thomas de Ludlow." (*Athenæum*, 13th June, 1894, p. 804.) A discussion on this follows.

held the Castles of Bamborough and Scarborough. Maitland's "Records of Parliament," 33 Ed. I.

Nicholaa de la Haye held Lincoln for the King. "And after the war it befell that the Lord the King (John) came to Lincoln, and the Lady Nicholaa came forth from the western gate of the castle, carrying the keys of the castle in her hand, and met the said Lord King John and offered him the keys as Lord; and said she was a woman of great age, and had endured many labours and anxieties in that castle, and she could bear no more. And the Lord the King returned them to her sweetly, and said, 'Bear them, if you please, yet awhile.'" This story appears in that Royal Commission of Inquiry into the condition of the country named the "Rotuli Hundredorum." The King was desirous to persuade so steadfast an adherent to continue to hold "in time of peace and in time of war" what, in those disturbed days, was one of the most important fortresses of the kingdom. For Nicholaa de la Haye, and Gerard de Camville her husband, had stood by King John in all his troubles; their attachment to him before he was King had brought suspicions and confiscations upon them. Gerard had to pay a heavy sum to Richard I. to be repossessed of his own estate, while Nicholaa paid the King three hundred marks for leave to marry her daughter to whom she would, provided it was not to an enemy of the King. After the death of Richard, Gerard de Camville was reinstated as Governor of Lincoln Castle, during the remainder of his life, and at his death John transferred the appointment to his wife, "a lady eminent in those days," says Dugdale. She continued at her post, and the King also appointed her Sheriff of Lincoln. In 1217 the partisans of Louis the Dauphin laid siege to Lincoln. Though the town sided with the besiegers, though 600 knights and 20,000 foot soldiers came to reinforce them, Nicholaa continued her defence of the castle till the Earl of Pembroke arrived with an army to her relief. In the next year she was again appointed Sheriff of Lincoln by Henry III. But this closed her public career, and she died in peace at Swaynston in 1229. ("Sketches from the Past," *Women's Suffrage Journal,* March, 1888.)

"Several Charters in one of the Duchy of Lancaster's Cowcher Books, prove that the Constableship of Lincoln-shire, the Wardenship of Lincoln Castle, and the Barony of Eye or Haia, always went together. They belonged successively to Robert de Haia, Richard de Haia, and Nicholaa de Haia, who became the wife of Gerarde de Camville." (Selby's "Genealogist," 1889, p. 170.) Lady Russell was appointed (in reversion), custodian of Donnington Castle for her life, at a salary of one pound and twopence - halfpenny a day. (*See* Privy Seal Warrants, March, 1589). Afterwards Queen Elizabeth granted the Castle itself to the Earl of Nottingham, and there was trouble over the right of residence. There were two suits. First, in the King's Bench, 1 James I. (Croke's Reports, 17 Jac.), and before the Star Chamber, 4 James I. (Sir Francis Moore's Law Cases, 1086). The lady was upheld in her grant.

"To Catherine de la Pole, Abbess of Barkyng, £50, for her costs about Edmund ap Meredith ap Tydier, and Jasper ap Meredith ap Tydier, lately committed to her custody by the King and Council." (*See* Issue Roll. Easter 17 Henry VI., 16th July.)

They could also be Justices of the Peace.—Nicholaa de la Haye acted as such *ex-officio* in the reign of John. In a book called "The Mirror of Justices," written about the reign of Edward II., a woman is spoken of as having been a Justice of the Peace. (This is referred to in Olive *v.* Ingram, 7, Mod. Rep., 267.) The wise and renowned Lady Margaret, Countess of Richmond, was made Justice of the Peace in the reign of Henry VII. (*See* Callis on Sewers, p. 251), and the Lady of Berkeley in the reign of Mary held the same office. In 5 Stephen Lucia, the Countess of Chester, paid a fine in the Exchequer, that she might do right among her tenants, that is, try them, and judge them without appeal. (*See* Madox, "History of the Exchequer," vol i., p. 397.*)

They could act as Femes Soles when married, or as

---

* The Bill for the qualification of women to sit on Borough and County Councils does not allow them to act as Justices of the Peace. Formerly, however, sex was no disqualification. There is still extant a note taken from the readings of Noy, the Attorney-General, in Lincoln's Inn, 1632, in which, on the question whether a woman might be justice of a forest, it was urged that Margaret, Countess of Richmond . . . Lady Berkeley . . . were Justices of the Peace, and that in Sussex, one Rouse, a woman, did usually sit upon the Bench at Assizes and Sessions among the other justices, *gladio cincta*, girded with a sword. (*See Daily Chronicle*, 5th June, 1907.)

Partners.—The Countess Lucy * was one of the few
Saxon heiresses that carried her property down into
Norman times. She had three Norman husbands, Ivo
de Tailleboys, Earl of Anjou, Roger Fitzgerald de
Romar, and Ranulph, Earl of Chester. Among the
various Charters to the Monastery of Spalding are two,
granting and confirming the grant of the Manor of Spalding to the Monks there. The exact words of the second
Charter are these : " I, Lucy Countess of Chester, give
and grant to the Church and Monks of St. Nicholas of
Spallingis with Soc and Sac, and Thol and Them, with
all its Customs, and with the liberties with which I best

* It is believed that Anglo-Saxon Earls had only official dignity
which was not hereditary. But the inheritance of the lands generally
carried the other privileges. Lucy was certainly made Countess of
Chester by her third husband, but in some authorities she is entitled
Countess of Bolingbroke, as in her own right. In Selby's
" Genealogist," 1889, there is a long discussion on the point, Who
was the Countess Lucy ? She is ordinarily considered the grand-
daughter of Leofric, Earl of Mercia (who died in 1057), and of his
wife, the famous Lady Godiva, who survived the Conquest. Their
son Alfgar, Earl of Mercia, twice rebelled against the Confessor,
and died in 1059. Lucy's two brothers were Edwin, Earl of
Mercia, and Morcar, Earl of Northumbria; her sister Edgiva married,
first, Griffith of Wales, and second, King Harold. Edwin and
Morcar were almost the only English nobles permitted by the
Conqueror to retain their lands. Lucy inherited much from her
father, probably with the Saxon privilege of the "youngest born,"
and afterwards more from her brothers. She married three Norman
husbands, with whom she held the position of a great heiress.
This is the view Dugdale takes. Others imagine, from her
longevity, there must have been two Lucys. The writer in " The
Genealogist " thinks, with good reason, that this Lucy was not the
daughter of Alfgar, but the only daughter and heiress of Thorold,
the Sheriff of Lincoln.

and most freely held in the time of Ivo Tailleboys and Roger Fitzgerald and the Earl Ranulph, my Lords, in almoign of my soul, for the Redemption of the soul of my father and of my mother, and of my Lords and relatives," etc. "Inspeximus by Oliver Bishop of London, 1284." (Selby's "Genealogist," pp. 70, 71.) In the lives of the Berkeleys, from the Berkeley MSS., 1883, published for the Bristol and Gloucester Archæological Society, some interesting particulars are given of the Lady Joane, daughter of Earl Ferrars and Derby, and wife of Lord Thomas of Berkeley, second of the name. "It appears by divers deeds that in the xxvith yeare of Edward the first, as in other yeares, this lady by hir deeds contracted with Richard de Wike and others as if she had been a *feme sole*; and for her seale constantly used the picture of herself holding in her right hand the escutcheon of her husband's arms, the chevron without the crosses; and in her left hand the escutcheon of her father's family, circumscribed Sigilla Johannæ de Berklai," vol i., p. 206.

Elizabeth, Lady of Clare, had buried three husbands, and had retained her maiden name through their time as holding the honour and the Castle of Clare,* in

---

* The petition of her "humble Chapeleyns Priour et chanoyns de sa priourie de Walsingham," that she would not allow the Franciscan friars to settle in their neighbourhood, is communicated by the Rev: James Lee-Warner of Norwich to the *Archæological Journal*, vol. xxvi., p. 167 (1869). One reason they bring forward is that if the intruders were to propose an indemnity, it could only be "par serment, ou par gages, ou par plegges," and that

Suffolk, which she inherited on the death of her brother, the last Earl of Gloucester and Hereford, at Bannockburn. Her daughter, Elizabeth de Burgh, married her cousin Lionel, third son of Edward III., in whom the Earldom of Clare became the Dukedom of Clarence.

In the Act of Resumption of 1 Henry VII., the King excludes the lands of his wife, his mother Cecile, Duchess of York, and others. And in the Act of Restitution of Margaret, Countess of Richmond, "she was to hold her lands as any other sole person, not wife, may do," though she was married at the time to the Earl of Derby. (Nos. 64 and 38 of the Private Acts, 1 Henry VII.)

Had the Cure of Churches.—The Abbesses of certain convents had the right of dominating the religious succession in some churches (Dyer in "Grimdon's Case," Plo. 496), "divers churches were appropriated to prioresses and nunneries, whereof women were the governesses" (Callis, 250). In the List of the Benefices of Wilton, 1383, I find (5) "The Church of St. Nicholas, Rector, The Abbess; The Church of Bulbridge, Rector, The Abbess" (Hoare's "Wiltshire," vol. i.). In Colt & Glover *v.* Bishop of Coventry and Lichfield about a presentation to a church, the evidence shows that many women before the Reformation had the Cure of churches; that an Archbishop could not legally appropriate a benefice with the Cure to a nunnery between 25 H.

such security is of no avail, as the claims of the apostolic See are beyond computation.

VIII., and the dissolution of monasteries, though the Pope did. (Hobart's Reports, pp. 140-148.)

"Mrs. Foulkes is the Lay-rector of Stanstey, and takes the tithes. She pays one shilling a year as quit-rent to the Lord of the Manor of Stanstey, County Denbigh" (Blount's "Tenures").

All appropriated churches shall have secular vicars. (*See* "Statutes of the Realm," vol. ii., 4 Henry IV., c. 12.)

Even by Dower they could inherit Office.—Women are dowable in a manor, an advowson, Tithes, Pensions, franchises, all tenures, liberties, profits, offices, as the office of a Bailiff or Parker (Co. Litt., 32ᵃ: F. N. B. 8, K. Marg.). "The ancient keepership of a park with a fee attached to it" (The Woman's Lawyer on Dower). The office of the Marshalsea of the King's Bench (21 Edward III., 57). (*See* also Co. Litt. as above.) In Hughes on Writs, p. 192, we find, "in every bailiwick or office in which the husband hath a fee, which bailiwick or office the wife may by herself or others sufficiently keep, she shall have Dower, but of the Steward or Marshal of England, which she cannot execute for herself, she shall not have Dower." She might, however, have by Dower the Custody of the gaol of Westminster Abbey, and many other high offices. (*See* J. J. Park on Dower.)

They could be Peeresses in their own Right and liable to Summons to Parliament in Person.—Sir Harris Nicolas says: "The usual form of a writ of summons to

Parliament is common. There is one solitary instance, however, of an express limitation of the dignity to heirs male, *i.e.*, in the Barony of Vesci " * (" Historic Peerages and Baronies by Writ "). In Lady Spenser's case (M. 11 Henry IV., f. 15) it was decided that it was clear law at all times that a Dame might be " Peer de Realm and entitled to all the privileges of such." † " All peers of the realm are looked on as the King's Hereditary Councillors " (*see* Jacob's " Law Dictionary ").

The opinions of Peeresses, as representing property, were always considered in the councils of the King. In the early Norman days they sat among the " Magnates Regni " in right of their fees and communities.‡ " In the Constitutions of Clarendon, Henry II., we find that ' Universæ Personæ Regni,§ qui de Rege tenent in Capite ' were to attend the King's Court and Council." (Report of the Lords' Committee on the Dignity of a Peer of the Realm.) The Abbesses,

---

* It is strange that this unique exception should have occurred in this barony, which had come through a woman, and had been held by a woman. Yvo de Vesci came over with William the Conqueror, and married Alda Tyson, daughter and heir of the Lord of Alnwick. Their daughter Beatrix was sole heir, and married Eustace of Knaresborough, their son taking his mother's name of De Vesci.

† *See* also " Statutes of the Realm," vol. ii., p. 321. Noble ladies shall be tried as peers of the realm are tried, when they are indicted of treason or felony (20 Henry VI., c. 9. Blackstone's " Commentaries," Bk. I., ch. xii.).

‡ *See* " Hiis Testibus " in Charters. Ant. Parl. 75.

§ *See* Stubbs's " Select Charters " (3rd Ed., pp. 137-140). Wharton's " Law Lexicon." S. W. Clarendon.

especially those of Shaftesbury, Barking, Wilton and St. Mary of Winchester, holding directly of the King, were summoned to Anglo-Norman Parliaments, as they had been summoned to Anglo-Saxon Witenagemots. Selden mentions their summons of 5 Edward I. as being extant in his time; their summons, twenty-nine years later, to the Parliament of 34 Edward I. is still extant, written in the same manner and terms as those of the other clergy. (Palgrave's "Parliamentary Writs"; 34 Edward I.)

Other peeresses were summoned according to their inheritance, which, we have seen, followed different lines from what it does to-day, or **by proxy.** By an exemption, intended as a privilege in those days of rough travelling and dangers, a peeress was permitted "to chuse and name her lawful proxy to appear for her *ad colloquium et tractatum coram rege* on her behalf." *

Alicia de Bigod sent her two proxies to Parliament, 35 Edward I. (*See* Rot. Parl., 189.) Selden and Gurdon mention "*nine* peeresses so summoned to the Parliament of 35 Edward III." There were in reality eleven. But there was not a *Parliament proper* that year, no writs having been issued for the Commons. It was rather a Council of Peers and Peeresses, especially of those holding lands in Ireland, who were summoned to consult with the King what should be done in that country, and what aid they would grant the King.

* Cited also by T. Chisholm Anstey in his "Supposed Constitutional Restraints," " Social Science," p. 293.

"Anno 35 Edward III., null. summoniciones 'but summons to council' 11 Comitissæ summonitæ ad mittend.
sede dignos ad. colloq." (Harl. MS., 6204, f. 167.)

"De consilio summonitæ pro Terras habentibus in
Hibernia 35 Edward III., Maria Comitissa Norfolk,
Elianora Comitissa Ormond, Anna le Despencer, Pha.
Comitissa de la Marche, Johanna Fitz Walter, Agnes
Comitissa Pembroch, Maria de Sancto Paulo Comitissa
Pembroch, Margeria de Ros, Matilda Comitissa Oxon,
Katherina, Com. Atholl, Nulla summonitio Parliamenti"
(Harl. MS., 778, f. 121). Dugdale gives the same names
("Summons to Parliament," p. 263) as summoned by
their faith and allegiance to send a deputy to consult with
the King and his council at Westminster. "Consimilia
Brevia diriguntur subscriptis, sub eadam Data, de
essendo coram Rege et consilio suo ad dies subscriptos,
viz., Ad Quindenam Paschæ Mariæ Comitissæ Norfolciæ,
Alianoræ Comitissæ de Ormond, Annæ le Despencer, Ad
tres Septimanas Paschæ Philippæ Comitissæ de la
March, Johannæ Fitz-Wauter, Agneti Comitissæ Pem-
brochiæ, Mariæ de S. Paulo Comitissæ Pembroc.,
Margeriæ de Roos, Matildæ Comitissæ Oxon, Katerinæ
Comitissæ Atholl, 35 Edward III., claus in dorso m. 36.
These because they had property in Ireland."

The proxies,* however, do not imply that the ladies
themselves would not have been admitted had they

---

* Francis Plowden notes on this : " So late even as 35 Edward
III. (1360), several Peeresses were summoned to Parliament . . .
they were called ad colloquium et tractatum by their proxies, a
privilege peculiar to the peerage." ("Jura Anglorum," p. 384.)

chosen to appear, as the special summons of Margaret, Countess-Marshal, in 1 Richard II., clearly proves. Men also were allowed to send proxies. "The Bishop of Bath and Wells being infirm and old is allowed to send a proxy to Parliament." "Ralph Botiller Miles, Lord of Sudeley, has the same permission" (6 Rot. Parl., app. ex Rot. Parl., 1 Edward IV., p. 1, m. [19] 227, a. b.).

The husband's succession to his wife's titles was in order to grant her a permanent and interested "proxy." In Dugdale's "Summons to Parliament," p. 576, there is "A catalogue of such noble persons as have had their summons to Parliament in right of their wives."

This proves :—

(1) That a man not entitled to be summoned in his own right could be summoned in his wife's right, but that in doing so he must take her name and title, whether higher or lower than his own : "George, son and heir to Thomas Stanley, Earl of Derby, having married Joane, the daughter and heir to John, Lord Strange of Knockin, had summons to the Parliament under the title of Lord Strange" (22 Edward IV., 1 Richard III., 3, 11, 12 Henry VII.).

(2) That a woman could hold her husband's titles and possessions till her death by the custom of England, and could even transfer these while she was alive to another husband. "Ralphe de Monthermer, having married Joane of Acre, daughter of King Edward I. and widow of Gilbert de Clare, Earl of Gloucester and Hertford, possessing lands of great extent in her right, which

belonged to these earldoms, had summons to Parliament from 28 Edward I. to 35 Edward I. by the title of Earl of Gloucester and Hertford. But after her death, which happened in the first year of King Edward the Second, he never had the title of Earl of Gloucester and Hertford, and was summoned to Parliament as a Baron only from the second to the eighteenth of that King's reign." (Dugdale's "Summons to Parliament.") There are twenty other cases of nobles summoned in the name of their wives. This, therefore, may be taken to illustrate the representative power in Peers. At the period of Ela of Salisbury the heiress of the Albemarles had conferred her title on three husbands, by the second of whom, William de Fortibus, she had an heir.

"Isobel of Gloucester likewise made her two husbands Earls." (Bowle's " History of Lacock Abbey.")

Margaret de Newburgh, Countess of Warwick, married John Marshall of the Pembroke family, and he became Earl of Warwick, *Jure Uxoris*. She re-married John de Plessetis, who also bore her title. Her cousin, William Mauduit, succeeded her, and then Isabel, his sister, who married William de Beauchamp, making him Earl of War-wick. Their daughter, Anne de Beauchamp, succeeded as Countess of Warwick. (Burke's " Extinct Peerages.")

Dugdale also mentions "the names of such noble persons whose titles are either the names of such heirs female, from whom they be descended, or the names of such places whence these heirs female assumed their titles of dignity : of whose summons to Parliament by these titles the general index will show the respective times." There are twenty-eight of them. The eldest sons of earls were sometimes summoned to Parliament by their father's second title in their father's lifetime, and these titles were often inherited from an ancestress.

That the right of Peeresses to be consulted in relation to aids or subsidies assessed on their property, was acknowledged, can be learned from interesting documents still preserved. "In the first year of Edward II., the King's collectors levied the subsidy on the goods and lands of Thomas Button, Bishop of Exeter, after his death, and it was resisted on the plea that he was never requested to pay the subsidy, nor agreed to do so. Several others used the like allegation '*quia non assensit*' and were thereon discharged by the court of Exchequer of the sums demanded of them ; for example, the Abbess of Shafton, the Prior of Bruton, and the Abbess of Godstow." (Placita coram Baronibus, 28 Edward III., Rot. 13, 27 Buk. Madox, 118.)

The Commons in 1404 voted a grant to the King (Rot. Parl., iii., 546). "La grante faite au Roy en Parlement. Vos pauvres Commons . . par assent des Seigneurs Spirituelx et Temporels . . grauntont à vous, en cest present parlement deux Quinzismes et deux Dismes pour estre levez des laie gentz, en manere accustume . . Et les Seigneurs Temporelx pur eux, et les *Dames Temporelx*, et toutz autres persones temporelx pour la depens suis dit grauntont . . . Et purtant que cestes subside soit grantez a vous . . lesqueux die soient

executy ne mys en œuvre avant la dit Quinzisme de
Seint Hiller q'alors ceste graunt entier soit voide et
tenue pur null ne levable, ne paiable en null manere
. . . Protestantz que ceste graunt en temps a venir ne
soit pris en ensample de charger les ditz Seigneurs et
Communes de Roialme . . sil ne soit par les voluntees
des Seigneurs et Communes de vostre Roiaume et ces de
nouvell graunt a faire en plein Parlement."

This, therefore, affirmed not only the rights of the
Ladies Temporal to be considered at the time, but the
grand principle of *De tallagio, non concedendo*, to all time
for all classes.

CHAPTER V

"Earls, Lords, and Ladies, Suitors at the County Courts."

THE Statutory history of Individual Privilege is not clear in very early times, before the Norman Customs and Saxon Laws coalesced. Magna Charta was wrested from John in 1215, and confirmed by succeeding monarchs. It is written in Latin, and the word Homo is applied throughout to both sexes. When it is intended to distinguish males from females other words are used. The most important clause in that Charter is, "To none will we sell, to none will we deny, to none will we delay the right of Justice." There were then no doubts in the mind of the people, no quibblings in the courts of law as to whether or not it extended to women. All early laws are couched in general terms, however they may have suffered from later legal and illegal glosses. Coke in his Institutes II., 14, 17, 29, and 45, explains that "Counts and Barons" represent all other titles, whether held by men or women; that Liber Homo meant *freeman and freewoman*. "Nullus liber homo. Albeit *homo* doth extend to both sexes, men and women, yet by Act of Parliament it is enacted and declared that this chapter should extend to Duchesses, Countesses, and Baronesses. Marchionesses and Viscountesses are omitted, but, notwithstanding, they are also comprehended within this chapter."

County women inherited freeholds under the same conditions as Noblewomen.

If an heiress married a man of an inferior family or a smaller property, she could, if she chose, raise him to her rank, and make him take her name. Thomas de Littleton, upon whose " Treatise on Tenures " Coke exercised his talents, received arms, name, and estate from his mother, "who, being of a noble spirit, *whilst it was in her power*, provided, by Westcote's assent, that her children should bear her name." In other words, the heiress of the Littletons married Westcote, but while she was yet a freewomen imposed conditions. (*See* " Life of Littleton " prefixed to Coke's Commentary.)

When married could act as femes soles.—Among "ancient deeds and charters, drawn up by landowners in the time of Edward III. and Richard II. " (Harl. MS. 6187), there are many executed by women, many sealed by women alone, their husbands being alive, many sealed by women along with their husbands.

A grant by William Faber de St. Briarville and Sarra his wife is sealed by the name of Sarra Hathwey alone, and another deed by her son is signed by William Faber, son and heir of Sarra Hathwey.

Robert de la Walter de Staunton and his wife Marjory combine in a deed, and the seals of both are affixed. So Thomas Waryn and his wife Julia, daughter of Thomas Baroun, Richard de Pulton and Agnes his wife, and others.

They owed also military service either to their Over-lord or to the King directly. We find this abundantly illustrated in Palgrave's "Parliamentary Writs," and in any of the Domestic Series of State Papers in the Public Record Office recording service assessed. All names are used in common. For instance, "Names of *gentle-men* furnishing light horses and lances, 1583 : Bramber, Dorothy Lewknor, 2 ; Pevensey, Elizabeth Pankhurst, 1, etc. ; Domina Gage, 2 ;* John Gage, 2 ; Elizabeth Geoffrey, 1 " (Harl. MS., 703, f. 87). "Names of the persons who did not appear at the musters of horsemen in Surrey, September, 1584." Among others with no note of difference were Mistress Frowman of Mitcham, widow ; Mistress Gresham, widow ; Mistress Gaynsford, widow (Dom. Ser. State Papers, Eliz., 173 [40]).

There are many women returned in the " Rotuli Hundredorum," Ed. I., as holding under military tenures in capite. " Eve de Stopham held her estate by finding for the King one footman, a bow without a string, and an arrow without feathers " (Blount's "Tenures "). "Lady Custance de Pukelereston holds Pukelereston by finding one man and a horse, with a sack and an axe, at the summons of the King" (" Testa

---

* These were "the two Gages" mentioned in connection with the Copleys of Gatton.

de Nevil," 252). The Manor of Gatton, known as the scene of contested elections in after years, was held by the service of a knight's fee and the payment of Castle guard to Dover Castle.

The " Testa de Nevil," compiled in the reign of Henry III. and Edward I., gives the list of many holding in capite and of Overlords by military service. " Margeria de Cauz has the gift of the lands of Sandford, held by the Serjeanty of keeping the Falcons of our Lord the King " (Berkshire Survey, " Testa de Nevil," Ed. III.)

They also paid and received Homage.—In the Harl. MS. (6187) many of the tenements are conveyed by women, on condition of Homage rendered and service given ; as, for instance, in the cases of Sibilla de Bruneshope, widow ; Johanna de Muchgross, daughter of William de Muchgross ; Agnes de Bellecores ; Agnes, daughter and heir of Henry de Munsterworth ; Cecilia Blundell de Teynton.

Among the Records of " Banham Marshall, Beckhall and Greyes," there is one transferring lands to a certain Dorothy Gawdy, 31st March, 1659. " At the court held by the Homagers "—" to which said Dorothy here in full courte is delivered thereof seisin. To hold to her and to her heires by A Rodd att the will of the Lords, according to the custom of this Manor, by the rents and services therefore due and of right accustomed and she giveth to the Lords a fine. Her fealty is respited for a certain time." Five days later this Lady died, and a new transfer was made to her heirs male in the same form.

They could present to Churches.—In 16 Edward II. Eleanor, wife of Thomas Multon of Egremond, petitions the King and Parliament against the Bishop for interfering with her appointment of a clerk, as she was endowed with the advowson of the Church of Natlugh in Ireland. Order that justice be done to the said Eleanor (Tower Rolls).

Matilda de Walda was patron by inheritance of Saint Michael's of Canterbury. (*See* "Rotuli Hundredorum," Edward I., vol. ii., 392.)

The Lady Copley presented to Gatton living in 1552.

The list, however, of ladies holding advowsons and gifts of churches is so long, that more need not be noted, especially as this right is not denied to-day.

They could hold Motes.—We may find the local duties of County women illustrated in the "Rotuli Hundredorum," and other authorities already quoted.

"Benedicta, widow of Sir Thomas Uvedale, granted a lease to Thomas Brown of 2½ acres and foure *dayewarcs* of land . . . by the yearly rent of 2s. 6d., and suit at her court of Wadenhalle every three weeks" ("Surrey Archæological Collection," vol. iii., p. 82).

They could attend Motes.

They could be free Suitors to the County Courts, and there act as Pares or Judges.—(*See* Prynne on the "Fourth Institute," xiii., 32, "Brevia Parl. Red." 431, mentioned by Probyn in Olive *v.* Ingram, 7 Mod. Rep. 268, quoted in T. C. Anstey's "Supposed Constitutional Restraints," 6 Edward I., c. i.) "*All* those who claim to have any franchises must appear at the Sheriff's Court to verify them. If they do not, they are distrained for non-appearance" (20 Henry III., c. x.). "Every freeman who oweth suit to County, trything, hundred, and wapentake, or to the court of his Lord may freely make his Attorney to do those suits for him."

Women combined with men to elect Knights of the Shire to defend in Parliament the rights of their property and themselves from unequal assessment of subsidy and undue exactions of the King.

In Sir Walter Raleigh's treatise on the Prerogative of Parliaments, he traces back the origin of the House of Commons to 18 Henry I. on rather slender bases. At the time of the struggle with John it was clearly perceived that irresponsible kings could not be trusted to observe all the clauses of Magna Charta, and general councils were provided for. John promised to summon *all classes* to consult with him when it was necessary to assess aids and scutage. But John's word was not worth much.

The first *clear* Summons appears to be that of 38 Henry III. (1254), when a Writ was issued requiring the Sheriff of each County to "cause to come before the King's Council two good and discreet Knights of the Shire, whom the *men* of the County shall have chosen for this purpose in the stead of all and of each of them, to consider, along with Knights of other Shires, what aid they will grant the King."

In 49 Henry III. (1265), writs were issued for * " two

* See Hallam's "State of Europe during the Middle Ages," p. 566.

Knights of the Shire to be chosen by *the annual suitors at the County Courts,*" and two Citizens from each Borough. Their expenses were to be paid by those who sent them.

The Statute passed in the Parliament of Marlebridge (52 Henry III.) by members elected in this manner, more clearly defined this method of election, and confirmed the more ancient Statutes regarding *the County Courts.* Hallam and Lewis trace their origin to the Anglo-Saxon Shiregemote, Folkmote, or Revemote, and prove that the Sheriffs and dignitaries possessed only directory and regulative powers; that the Freeholders, who were obliged to do "suit and service," were the Pares or Judges, as well as the Electors of the Knights of the Shire, and of the Sheriffs themselves.

Concerning this court, it had been provided (43 Henry III., c. x.) "that no Archbishops, Bishops, Earls, Barons, nor any religious Men or Women, should be obliged to come thither unless their presence was especially required." Their goods could not be distrained for non-attendance. That this was intended as a Franchise of Privilege, not inducing a penalty of exclusion, is perfectly clear, not only in the reading of the Act itself, but in its effect upon later laws.

Coke (Inst. II., 119), elucidating the laws of Marlebridge, made nine years later, says : "Note.—A woman may be a free Suitor to the Courts of the Lord, but though it be generally said that the free suitors be Judges in these courts, it is *intended of men and not of women.*"

F

This "priestly intention" sprang only from Coke's own mind. He cites no authority for his opinion, nor could he have found one. To have deprived a female "Suitor" of her right to express her opinion, and thereby help to determine the questions brought before the Court, in the light of her own interests, inclinations, or opinions, would have taken away her prime *raison d'être.* Her second privilege was that of giving her voice, with other freeholders, towards the election of a knight, "in the stead of all and of each of them," to go to the King's Parliament,* and defend her interests there. Upon the petition of the Commons that proclamation should be made of the day and place of the meeting of the County Court, it was decreed : "All they that be there present, as well *suitors* duly summoned, as *others,* shall attend to the election of the Knights for the Parliament . . . And after they be chosen, the names of the persons so chosen shall be written in an *Indenture,*† under the *seales* of all them that did chuse them, and tacked to the said writ of Parliament" (7 Henry IV., c. xv.). A certain limitation, therefore, of electors, must have been caused through the necessity of possessing seals. By 8 Henry VI., c. vii., the suitors at the County Court were limited to those who had not less than a 40s. freehold. It was

---

* The first use of the word "Parlement" occurs in the Prologue to the Statute of Westminster in 3 Edward I. (1275).

† Prynne notes that only Cedules have been preserved of the returns of the knights before the Statute of 7 Henry IV., c. xv. "The Indenture shall be holden for the Sheriff's return " (4th Inst., 10, 48).

soon made clear that the House of Commons was only intended to represent those not eligible in person or in representation to the Upper House; so that the county elections became limited to county freeholders below the rank of Peers. But there is no question, at any time, of altering the Franchise from the general terms to others that would limit it to the masculine being. That women did frequent the courts in person is proved in Prynne's "Brevia Parliamentaria Rediviva" (p. 152, *et seq.*), where he refers to "sundry Earls, Lords and Ladies who were annual suitors to the County Courts of Yorkshire." That women recorded these votes, and sealed the indentures of the Knights elected, is also proved by Prynne. The two points that surprised Prynne were, that the earliest preserved indentures were *all* signed by the Nobility of the County, and by them alone, and also that they were all sealed by attorney, by Lords, or by Ladies alike, down to 7 Henry VI., after which they were signed by all Freeholders personally. He does not seem to remember that these were the classes privileged by Act 43 Henry III., to absent themselves from the County Courts; and that acting by proxy was considered a privilege of the nobility. It might very well have been considered that Archbishops, Earls, Lords, and Ladies were "especially required" at the County Court to hear and decide on some important territorial dispute, and yet that they could decide on the merits of a candidate at home, and send their Attorneys to the County Court to seal for them there in the presence of the Sheriff. One such indenture (2 Henry V.) is signed by Robert Barry, the Attorney of Margaret, widow of Sir Henry Vavasour. (*See* Samuel Heywood's "Law of County Elections," pp. 160-2.) In another return from the County of York, one Attorney signs for the Earl of Westmoreland, and another for the Countess, for the lands each held as freeholds in that neighbouring county.

Prynne also preserves an Indenture signed by the attorney of Lucia, the widowed Countess of Kent (13 Hen. IV.). (Returns to Parliament, 13 Hen. IV. to 12 Ed. IV.; Prynne's "Brev. Parl. Red.," pp. 152-5.) This lady was an Italian, a Visconti, the daughter of the Duke of Milan, and her foreign extraction, or her failing fortunes at the time,* may have induced her to exercise her privilege as regards the Member of Parliament, while she preserved the dignity of her nobility by voting by Attorney.

There are not so many examples of women voting as we would like. But it has been noted that many of the writs are lost. "What if they had all been lost, embezzled, or made away with? What, then, is our Constitution lost, when bundles of writs are lost?" (Bell's "History of Magna Charta," p. 138.)

"The Franchises of the land . . . every Englishman, by being born into the land, is born unto them, transmitted to us by the hard labour of our ancestors, they are the children's bread." (*Ibid.*, p. 95.)

---

* *See* Petitions to Parliament (Hen. IV.), Burke's "Extinct Peerages," "Inquisitions *Post-Mortem.*" (Hen. V.)

I have not found any example of a lady "Knight of the Shire," but neither have I found the shadow of a *law* against her existence beyond that of the electors' choice, or the lady's convenience. Anne Clifford said that if her candidate did not come forward "she would stand herself." (Dr. Smith to Williamson, Jan. 1668. Dom. Ser. State Papers, Public Record Office.) But as women summoned to do military service were *allowed* to send a substitute, as women summoned to the County Courts were *allowed* to absent themselves, and *allowed* to send an Attorney, so were they allowed to send their knights to the House of Commons.

"Lady Freeholders occur in the Official Lists for Dumfriesshire in the seventeenth century. Did they exercise the right of voting for members of Parliament?" ("Notes and Queries," 4th Series, VI., 175.)

If women of the Middle Ages had but realised what their ancestresses did before them, "that they were receiving what they must hand down to their children neither tarnished nor depreciated, what future daughters-in-law may receive, and may so pass on to their grand-children" (Tacitus, "Germ.," c. xviii.), the needs of litigation on this point might not have arisen later.

In relation to women's attendance at Manorial Courts, where they were among the jury to decide on local cases, it is evident that they were not only allowed, but summoned to attend, and failing a proxy or just excuse, were fined. (*See* Blackstone's "Commentaries," vol. i., p. 178 ; Reeve's "History of the English Law," vol. i., p. 47.)

Could Nominate to Private Boroughs. — Certain Boroughs formerly held by military tenure seem to have been included in those permitted to return burgesses to Parliament, though belonging to one owner. When women inherited the property and held the Borough, they returned their one or two members, as the custom might be, in their own name. "The members of many ancient Boroughs were often returned by the Lords, and sometimes by the Ladies of the Manors or Boroughs" (Plowden's "Jura Anglorum," p. 438). Many cases are doubtless lost among the piles of missing records. But two very illustrative examples have been preserved for us, just sufficient to clear away all doubts from the minds of students of history, that women sometimes exercised the privileges they possessed. (T. C. Anstey's "Sup. Parl. Restraints," p. 19.)

In a bundle of Returns for 14 and 18 Eliz., Brady has preserved, and Heywood, in his "County Elections," has quoted, that of Dame Dorothy Packington, the owner of the private Borough of Aylesbury. (*Cited* by C. J. Lee in Olive *versus* Ingram, 7 Mod. Rep. 263, 271.) In days when military service might have been demanded of her, she would have sent her "substitute" to defend her sovereign; in days when subsidy service was expected of her, she sent a "substitute" to Parliament to defend her interests there, and she paid for both her military and civil representatives. "To all Christian people to whom this present writing shall come, I,

Dame Dorothy Packington, widow, late wife of Sir John Packington, Knight, Lord and Owner of the Town of Aylesbury, sendeth greeting. Know ye me, the said Dame Dorothy Packington, to have shown, named, and appointed my trusty and well-beloved Thomas Lichfield and John Burden, Esquires, to be my burgesses of my said Town of Aylesbury. And whatsoever the said Thomas and John, burgesses, shall do in the service of the Queen's highness in that present parliament to be holden at Westminster the 8th day of May next ensuing the date hereof, I, the same Dame Dorothy Packington, do ratify and approve to be my own act, as fully and wholly as if I were, or might be present myself." She signed their indentures, sealed them, paid "their wages" and their expenses in whole, as others did in part. That the return was held good is sufficient to prove its legality.* There is not the shadow of grounds for a belief that she "acted as returning officer," as some have said who have not studied the case. Later on, when the population of Aylesbury increased, and the ambitions of Aylesbury extended, there was an appeal by the inhabitants for permission to share in the Returns.† But the objection to the monopoly of the

---

* *See* List of Parliamentary Returns, vol. i., p. 487.

† A trial in Aylesbury because some inhabitants brought a case against the Mayor and Constables as returning officers for refusing their vote, saying that "refusing to take the plaintiffs' vote was an injury and damage." (Jacob's "Law Dictionary." Ashby *versus* White, 14 State Trials, 6th January, 1700, 695, 1 Smith's Leading Cases, S.C.)

Family - Return did not include an objection to the woman that exercised it.

Another memorable instance is preserved for us in the Journals of the House of Commons itself.

I have found out so many curious, hitherto unnoted details about it, that I thought it advisable fully to illustrate the conditions of the case, so that it may not again be mistranslated, as it has so often been. On 25th March, 1628, there was a contested election for the Borough of Gatton. There were *two* indentures returned, one by the inhabitants of the borough, and the other by Mr. Copley. Though he returned Sir Thomas Lake and Mr. Jerome Weston, " it was held not good that he should have returned alone." The case was argued out before the Committee of Privileges in the House of Commons, of which Glanville, Hake-well, and Sir Edward Coke were members. Mr. Copley based his claim on returns made by Roger Copley, as the *sole inhabitant* in 33 Henry VIII.; and by Mrs. Copley in 1 and 2 Phil. and Mary, 2 and 3 Phil. and Mary. " On the other part, in 7 Edward VI., Mrs. Copley et omnes inhabitantes returned. In 28°, 43° Eliz. and 1°, 18° Jac., the return was made by the inhabitants, and in all later parliaments Mr. Copley joined with the other inhabitants."

The Committee and the other members of the House decided that " Mrs. Copley and the other inhabitants " was the true and legal Precedent for the form of Return. And that is the last word Parliament has had to say upon a Woman-Elector. (*See Commons' Journal* of date.) But the side-lights of the story are interesting. In the first place, the *Commons Journal* has a misprint of an "s" in two cases. Roger Copley died in 1550-1; and from the manuscript copies of the *Commons Journal* we may see that *Mrs.* Copley is entered as returning alone in 1 and 2 Philip and Mary, and 2 and 3 Philip and Mary. (*See* Lansdowne MS., 545.) Further, both the printed and the MS. copy are wrong about her title, as she was the Dame Elizabeth Copley, or "Elizabeth Copley, Domina de Gatton." This mistake shows that her own *seal* was affixed to the indenture with her Christian name, to which the Committee added "Mrs." instead of Dame or "Lady." Further, she must also have returned in 4 and 5 Philip and Mary, and must have returned her son.* On the 5th March young Copley of Gatton was committed to the sergeant for irreverent words spoken of Her Majesty, and on 7th March Parliament was prorogued till 5th November. (*Commons' Journal.*) This receives further explanation in Additional MS. 24, 278, collected by Sir Richard St. George Norroy :—" Saturday 5th March, 4 and 5 Philip and Mary. For that Mr. Copley, a member of this House, hath spoken irreverent words of the Queene's Majestie, concerning the Bill for confirmacion of pattents, saying that he feared the Queene might thereby give away the Crowne from the

---

* "Thomas Copley Armiger, Thomas Norton Armiger, Gatton." Names supplied from the Crown Office in place of original returns. (Parliamentary Returns, vol. i., p. 398.)

right inheritor, the House commanded, by Mr. Speaker, that Copley should absent himself until consultation more had thereof. And after consultation had and agreed to be a grievous fault, Copley was called in and required this House to consider his youth, and that if it be an offence it might be imputed to his young yeares. The House referred the offence by the Speaker to the Queene with a plea for mercy, and Mr. Copley committed to the custody of the Sergeant-at-arms. Monday, 7th March, Mr. Speaker declared that he had declared to the Queene's Majestie the matter touching Copley, wherein hir pleasure was that he should be examined whereof fresh matter did spring. Nevertheless, Her Majestie would well consider the request of the House in his favour. In the afternoon Parliament prorogued " (*Commons' Journal*). "Elizabeth, the second wife and widow of Sir Roger Copley, daughter of Sir William Shelley, Justice of the Common Pleas, presented to the Church of Gatton in 1552, as did her son Thomas in 1562; but after that time, the family, being Roman Catholics, it was vested in trustees, 1571 " (Manning and Bray's "Surrey"). The troubles of the Copleys and Gatton arose from *recusancy*, not from women's elections. Elizabeth died in 1560, "seized of Gatton," held of the Queen in fealty for 1d. rent, and 20s. castle-guard to Dover Castle. (*See* "Inquisition *Post-Mortem*," 29th April, 2 Eliz.) It must, therefore, have been settled on herself. The daughter of Sir William Shelley would surely be well advised of her legal rights, and perhaps her association of the other inhabitants with herself in her election of 7 Edward VI. arose from an appreciation of the tendency of popular opinion in favour of an inhabitant suffrage, instead of a freeholding one, or from some sense of the need of the protection of numbers to a *recusant*.

In Harl. MS., 703, Burghley writes to the Sheriff of Surrey:—"Whereas there are to be returned by you against the Parliament two Burgesses for Gatton in that Countie of Surrey, which, *heretofore*, have been *nominated by Mr. Copley*, for that there are no Burgesses in the Borough there to nominate them, for as much as by the death of the said Mr. Copley and minoritie of his sonne, the same which his lands are within the survey and rule of the Court of Wards, whereof I am her Majestie's chiefe officer, you shall, therefore, forbeare to make returne of anie for the saide towne, without direction first had from me therein, whereof I praie you not to faile" (St. James, 13th November, 1584). Sir Thomas died abroad, 1584, aged 49, leaving William, his son and heir. Apparently Francis Bacon and Thomas Busshop had been nominated by Burghley; because the next letter preserved, dated 24th November, 1584, tells the Sheriff to appoint Edward Browne, Esq., in the place of Bacon, who had been returned for another borough. On 11th September, 1586, Walsingham instructs the Sheriff of Sussex to send up Mrs. Copley of Rossey to the charge of the Warden of the Fleet, and the two Gages, and they are to have no conference.

January 29th, 1595, Buckhurst writes to Sir Walter Covert and Harry Shelley, Esq., to apprehend " the Lady Copley and certaine other daungerous persons remayning with her as it is enformed, where very dangerous practizes are in hande" (Harl. MS. 703, f. 87).

" The Queen, by reason of —— Copley, Esq., going beyond sea and not returning according to Parliament, presented Ralph Rand, M.A., to the Church of Gatton, 8th February, 1598."

On 7th February, 1620, the House considered the return of Gatton in Surrey. One Smith, a burgess for that town, and a son of Mr. Copley, appeared. Mr. Copley, lord of the town, a recusant convict, with six of his lessees, no freeholders, made their choice the Tuesday before ; the freeholders made their choice, on the Wednesday, of Sir Thomas Gresham and Sir Thomas Bludder. The first return held void. Sir Henry Brittayne asked leave to speak ; he said " the writ was directed Burgensibus, and delivered to Mr. Copley. The town was but of seven houses, all but one Copley's tenants. That the election by them good not being freeholders. That all the freeholders, except one, dwelt out of the town, and only held of the manor in the town." " Sir Edward Coke spoke against Copley's return, and moved for a new election, *in case of danger from Copley*" (*Commons' Journal*). (*See* also Lansd. MS., 545 ; Hakewell's " Report of the Gatton Case.")

This, therefore, makes the controversy comprehensible that, in 1628, was illustrated by the records.

Mr. William Copley was not inclined tamely to resign the ancient privilege of his family of sending up Burgesses for their own Borough ; he attempted to do so again, in spite of the decision of 1620, and through the adverse decision in his case, Parliament affirmed, and Sir Edward Coke with it, the right of a woman to vote.

CHAPTER VI

FREEWOMEN

" Preserve your Loyalty, defend your Rights."
Anne Clifford's Sundial Motto.

IN days when the word " Free " had no doubtful signifi-
cation, women could be " Free " in several different
ways.   They could be freeholders in the country on
comparatively small estates, and were liable to be
summoned to the Manorial Courts of the Lords or
Ladies from whom they held their land.   If they did
not appear, send a proxy, or a valid excuse, they were
liable to be fined.   In looking through the Records of
Rowington, for my special work on Shakespeare, I found
among the list of those fined " Joan Shakespeare for
default of suit of court, 4d."   The same sum is
charged to male absentees.

They could be Freeholders in towns by inheritance or
by purchase.   They could be Free of " Companies," in
some of them by patrimony, service, or payment ; in
others only through being widows of Freemen.
In some cases a widow's " Freedom " was limited
by the conditions of her husband's will, but in almost all

94

of the Companies, at least in London, *some* women could be Free. They could be Free in other Boroughs, under the same conditions as men, by paying brotherhood money, and by sharing in the common duties of Burgesses, as " Watch and Ward," "Scot and Lot," and the service of the King; they could be " Free " as regards the Corporation, and they could be " Free " as regards voting for members of Parliament.

I have preferred to use the word "Freewomen" as more definite than any other. The " Widows and Spinsters' " phrase of to-day does not carry back to old history. Under certain limited conditions married women could be "Free"; under certain other conditions they could be " Spinsters."

" The case of a wife trading alone. And where a woman coverte de Baron follows any craft within the city by herself apart, with which the husband in no way interferes, such woman shall be bound as a single woman as to all that concerns her craft. And if the husband and wife are impleaded in such case, the wife shall plead as a single woman in a Court of Record, and shall have her law and other advantages by way of plea just as a single woman." She has her duties and penalties as well as her privileges,* can be imprisoned for debt, etc. (*See*

---

* One of these was a choice of her jury, whether of men or of women. There are numerous instances in old records of women acting as Compurgators or Jury, at least in women's cases. "On 1st February, 1435, Parochia Edlyngeham, Margareta Lyndseay contra Johannem de Longcaster, Johannem Somerson, Johannem Symson, Diflamata quod fuit incantatrix . . . negavit et purgavit se cum Agnete

"The Liber Albus of London," compiled 1419, translated by J. Riley, Book III., p. 39.)

(*See* also "Historical Manuscripts Commission," vol. x., Appendix iv., p. 466, *et. seq.* Report on papers found in Town Hall, Chelmsford.) There, among several lists of women, wives, and mothers, are many designated "Spinsters." Among "presentments for neglecting to attend church" (23 Eliz.) were ten women—"Margareta Tirrell, spinster, alias dicta Margaretta Tirrell uxor Thomae Tirrell armigeri"; "Maria Lady Petre, spinster, alias dicta Maria Domina Petre uxor Johannis Petre de Westhornden prædicta Militis." Many others appear as "wife of" at the same time as "spinster." The writer of the Report believes that "spinster" in these cases was equivalent to "generosa," and notes that it is insisted on when women have married men of meaner descent. I myself am inclined to think that a Guild of women had arisen out of the silk-spinning industries of Essex, and that the word "Spinster" implied membership of that Guild.

Members of Guilds.—In the old social and religious guilds which seem to have been established for good-fellowship during life, for due burial, prayers and masses

Wright, Christiana Ansom, Alicia Faghar, Emmota Letster, Alicia Newton, et restituta est ad famen, et Johannes Longcaster, Johannes Somerson, Johannes Symson, moniti sunt sub pœna excommunicationis quod de cetero talia non prædicent de ipsa:"

On 3rd October, 1443, "Beatrix Atkynson and Margareta Donyll habent ad purgandum se cum 6th manu mulierum honestarum vicinarum suarum" ("Depositions from the Court of Durham. Surtees Society," p. 28, 29). (*See* also "Liber Albus.")

after death, and for charitable assistance of needy sur-
vivors, there was perfect equality between the sexes.
Brotherhood money is exacted from "the sustren" as
well as from the brethren. In 1388 (12 Richard II.) an
order was given that all Guilds and Brotherhoods should
give "returns of their foundation." Women appear as
the Founders of some of these. The Guild of the
Blessed Virgin Mary, Kingston-upon-Hull, was founded
by 10 men and 12 women ("Early English Gilds," J.
Toulmin Smith, p. 155). The Guild of Corpus Christi,
Hull, founded in 1358, by 18 women and 25 men
(p. 160). The Guild of the Holy Cross, Stratford-on-
Avon, had half of its members women, as also the Guild
of Our Lady, in the Parish of St. Margaret's, Westminster, whose original manuscripts I have read. Even
when the guild was managed by priests, as in the Guild
of Corpus Christi, York, women were among the
members. In St. George's Guild, Norwich, men were
charged 6s. 8d. and women only 3s. 4d. for brotherhood.
These guilds had "Livery" of their own in some cases.
They had a beneficial effect on society, moral good
conduct being necessary to membership, and a generous
rivalry in self-improvement a condition of distinction.
They taught an equal moral standard for both sexes.
Hence the treatment of vicious men and vicious women
was the same. (*See* "Liber Albus," pp. 179, 180, etc.)

They also did many good works towards the public
weal.

The Guild of the Holy Cross in Birmingham, to

G

which belonged the well-disposed men and women of Birmingham and the neighbouring towns, had Letters Patent in 1392. The Report of its Condition in the reign of Edward VI. says : " It kept in good reparacions two great stone Bridges and divers foule and dangerous wayes, the charge whereof the town, of hitselfe ys not hable to manteign, so that the lacke thereof will be a great noysaunce to the Kinges Majesties subjects passing to and from the marches of Wales, and an utter ruyne to the same towne, being one of the largest and most profitable townes to the Kinges Highness in all the Shyre" (Toulmin Smith's " English Gilds," pp. 244-249).

These might have weathered the storms of the Reformation by giving up candles and masses, had not Henry seized their revenues and revoked their foundations.

The Trades' Guilds in early days were also semi-religious in their character, and also admitted women as sisters.

William Herbert's " History of the Twelve Great Livery Companies" gives many details interesting to us. All the Charters of the Drapers' Company expressly admit Sisters with full rights ; the wearing of the Livery, the power of taking apprentices, sitting at the election feasts, making ordinances among themselves for better governance, etc. (vol. i., p. 422). So also did the Clothworkers.

So also the Brewers' Company. In 5 Henry V there were 39 women on the Company's Livery paying full quarterage money. In 9 Henry V. there are entries in the books, of the purchase of cloth for the clothing of the Brethren and Sistren of the Fraternity of the Brewers' Craft. So also the Fishmongers (p. 59), the Weavers,* and other companies.

The Armourers' Company held women freemen. (*See* the old lists of the Freemen of the City of London at Guildhall Library.) "The office of Plumber of the Bridge granted to the Widow Foster, 1595." (Guildhall Records.)

The Clockmakers' Company, though only founded in 1632, had female apprentices sanctioned by the company so late as 1715, 1725, 1730, 1733, 1734, and 1747.

Among the Memoranda of the Grocers' Company, 1345, we may note "each member of the fraternity shall bring his wife or his companion to the dinner." "And that all the wives that now are, and afterward shall become married to any of our Fraternitie; they shall be entered and esteemed as belonging to the Fraternitie *for ever* to assist them and treat them as one of us, and after the decease of her husband the widowe shall still come to the said election dinner, and shall pay 4od. *if she be able.* And if the said widow is married to some other, who is not of our Fraternitie, she shall not come to the said dinner so long as she be 'couverte de Baroun,' nor ought any of us to meddle with her in anything, nor interfere on account of the Fraternitie so long as she is 'couverte de Baroun.'"

* *See* "Liber Customarum," p. 544, etc.

(*See* Mr. Kingdon's translation of the Books of the
Grocers' Company, 1341-1463, printed in 1886.) On a
second widowhood she might return to the company.
At a later date they did not seem to be so severe. One
widow, interesting to me on other literary grounds, made
her second and third husbands free of the company
through the rights she gained from her first. Widows
paid Brotherhood money, held Apprentices, traded and
received all benefits of the Guild. There may have
been spinster daughters among them also. In vol. ii.,
p. 328, I found a note of "Sarah Whitten's admission."

"23rd December, 1556.—Henry Bett's widow married
one Pasmore, who asks leave to keep on her apprentices."

"10th April, 1557.—Thomas Twyrtyn, late apprentice
with Margaret Foster, widow, to be made free."

"Brotherhood Money. — 1543," Wydow Holtham
heads the list, 2s.; "1554, Mrs. Bodley, 2s.; Alice
Alstropp, 12d.; Mrs. Byttenson, 2s.; Mrs. Blagge,
2s.," etc.

The Company of Stationers seems to have followed
similar customs. Many women carried on their
husbands' businesses, and received apprentices, as
Widow Herforde, Widow Alldee, Widow Field. (*See*
Arber's reprint of "Stationers' Registers" and Ames'
"Typographical Antiquities.")

In the "Journal of the House of Commons," vol. ii.,
p. 331, 3rd December, 1641, we find two entries,
"Ordered that the Committee for printing do meet
to-morrow at eight of the clock in the Inner Court

of Wards, and the printing of the Book of Queries is referred to that Committee."

"Ordered that Elizabeth Purslow, who, as this House is informed, printed the pamphlet entitled 'Certain Queries of some Tender-Conscienced Christians,' be summoned to attend the Committee appointed to examine the business."

In Timperley's "Cyclopædia of Literary Typographical Anecdote" we find: In 1711 died Thomas James, a noted printer in London, according to Dunton, "something the better known for being husband to that She-State politician, Mrs. Eleanor James." This extraordinary woman wrote two letters to printers, one to Masters, and one to Journeymen, the first beginning, " I have been in the element of printing above forty years," and ending, " I rest your sister, and soul's wellwisher, Eleanor James." Her husband, Thomas James, left his fine library to the use of the public, and the President and Fellows of Sion College were indebted to Mrs. James for giving them the preference. She also presented them with her own portrait, with that of her husband, and his grandfather, Thomas James, first librarian to the Bodleian Library. " Her son, George James, who died in 1735, was City Printer. His widow carried on the business for some time, when the office was conferred on Henry Kent." (Timperley; *see* also Reading's "Catalogue of Sion College Library.")

The Barber-Surgeons' Company, from the earliest times until now, has been open to women, and they bound their apprentices, boys and girls, at the Common Hall. (*See* Mr. Sydney Young's " History of the Company.")

Women could also have Guilds of their own.*—In 3 and 4 Edward IV., there was a " Petition from the Silke-women and Throwsters of the Craft and occupation of Silkework within the cite of London, which be, and have been craftes of women within the same cite of tyme that noo mynde renneth to the contrarie, nowe more than a M " (*i.e.*, 1,000 in number), praying protection against the introduction of foreign manufactured silk goods. (Parliamentary Rolls, 1463, vol. v., p. 506.) And various Acts for their protection are passed, down to 19 Henry VII., c. xxi.

There seems also to be somewhat of the nature of a Guild among the Midwives of London, who had a certain social standing, and certain laws and conditions of office. Many of the Royal Midwives received annuities. One appears in Rot. Parl. XIII. Ed. IV., vol. vi., p. 93. Among the exclusions from the Act of Resumption we find, " Provided alwey that this Act extend not, nor in any wise be prejudiciall to Margery Cobbe, late the wyf of John Cobbe being midwyf to our

---

* Ed. III. imposed limitations upon men's labour, but left women the privilege to work free. " Mais l'intention du roi et de son conseil est que femmes, cestassavoir brasceresces, pesteresces, texteresces, fileresces, et œvresces si bien de layne come de leinge, toille, et de soye, brandestesters, pyneresces de layne et totes autres que usent œveront œveraynes manuels puissent user et œverer franchement come els ont fait avant ces hures sanz mal empeschement ou autre restreint par ceste ordeignance." (Rot. Parl., 37 Ed. III., c. vi.) This is important in relation to modern legislation about women's freedom to labour.

best-beloved wyfe Elizabeth Queen of England, unto any graunte by us, by owre Letters Patentes of £40 by year, during the Life of the said Margery." Even in early times, their male rivals tried to limit the extent of their professional activities. Among the Petitions to Parliament is one from Physicians who pray that "no woman be allowed to intermeddle with the practice of Physic." (I. Rot. Parl., 158.ᵃ *See* also Petition, 9 Henry V. 142.)

The Rolls of the Hundreds make mention of women among the great Wool Merchants of London, "Widows of London who make great trade in Wool and other things, such as Isabella Buckerell and others" (vol i., pp. 403-4).

They might be Free of the City of London.—The freedom of the city of London became vested in those that paid Scot and Lot, as women did. The Jews were not allowed to pay Scot and Lot, and were never "free of the city." "And the King willeth that they shall not, by reason of their Merchandize, be put to Scot or Lot, or in any taxes with the men of the cities or Boroughs where they abide; for that they are taxable to the King as his bondmen, and to none other but the King. ("Statutes of the Realm," vol. i., p. 221. Les Estatuz de la Jeurie. Ruffhead's Statutes, vol. ix., App., p. 28). "That all Freemen shall make contribution unto taxes and taillage in the city" ("Liber Albus," III., pt. i., 235). "For watch and ward. Let all such make contribution as shall be hostelers and housekeepers in each ward"

(p. 102). "And the *Freeman*, when *she is a woman*, shall have no excuse from the duties of watch and ward." "And deeds and indentures, and other writings under seal may be received; and cognizances and confessions of women as to the same recorded before the Mayor and one Alderman" (p. 16). "Where women in such cases (*i.e.*, of debts) are impleaded and wage their law," they make their law with men or women at their will (p. 37).

Walter *v.* Hanger.   Sir Francis Moore's Cases, 832. Pasch., 9 Jac. I. Frances Hanger. "El plead que el fuit libera fœmina de London, et plead le Charter," 1 Ed. II., that "the Freemen of London should pay no dues upon their wines." These points are important to remember in the light of a petition presented by the widows of London (17 Richard II.) to be freed from taxes and taillage made in the city without authority of Parliament; praying the king to remember that it had been granted them that no such tax would be imposed; and asking him to see that this present Parliament would prevent the Mayor and Sheriff of London from levying on them this new imposition not levied by Act of Parliament. (Rot. Parl., vol. iii., 325.) The Mayor and Aldermen present a counter petition saying that the tax was for restorations, and praying that the present Parliament should ordain that the widows may be contributors according to proportion of the aforesaid fine, for their tenements and rents in the city and suburbs according to right and reason, ancient custom and charters of the city, that those who *per commune* have advantage of the restoration ought by right to be contributors in cost, etc. (*Ibid.*).*

That women were no indifferent and over-timid members of the community, we may see in the petition of the Mercers of London to the King against the oppressions of Nicholas Brember, Grocer and Mayor of London, 1386, 10 Richard II. :—

"Also we have be comaunded ofttyme up owre ligeance to unnedeful and unleweful loose doynges. And also to withdrawe us be the same comandement fro things nedeful and leeful, as was shewed when a company of gode women, there men dorst nought, travailled en barfote to owre lige Lorde to seeke grace of hym for trewe men as they supposed, for thanne were such proclamacions made that no man ne woman shold

* A charter was granted for "the Exemption of the Widows of London, from Talliages Redemptions, Contributions, according to the free customs they have had during our reign and that of our predecessors, that they be not harassed or troubled by any impositions, 19th June, 52 Henry III." (Guildhall Records, c.f. 28). "Widows of London. Maire, Aldermen, et Communaultee, Relevacion—*i.e.*, they petition that the present Parliament should ordain that the widows may be contributors according to the proportion of the Fine undernamed, for their tenements and rents in your City and the Suburbs, in manner and form aforesaid, according to right and reason, the ancient customs of the city, and the effect of the Charter aforesaid, notwithstanding. Having consideration, most gracious sir, that all those, who, *per commune* have advantage of the Kingdom or of the City, ought by right to be contributors in cost upon these facts, or otherwise there would follow final destruction to cities in case of sieges or in famine, or other similar cases." (17 Richard II., Rot. Parl.)

approche owre lige Lorde for sechynge of grace, etc."
(Rot. Parl., vol. iii., p. 225.)

They could be Free in other Boroughs.—The female
burgesses of Tamworth are recorded in Domesday Book
as having been free before the Conquest, and as being
still free in later times. If they took it upon them
to trade as *femes soles*, they made themselves liable
to all the common burdens of the "mercheta," over
and above their proper borough duties of watch and
ward.

The Ipswich Domesday Book gives more than one
instance of a woman having "hominal rights," and as
being liable to the "hominal duties" corresponding
thereto. To any *feme sole* the Franchise, and even the
Guild, was open on the same terms as to the men of the
place. There was no essoign (excuse) of female burgesses
in Ipswich whereby to decline attendance at the motes
(30 Edward I.). These references to the "Ipswich
Dom. Boc." are from T. Chisholm Anstey's "Supposed
Constitutional Restraints," p. 21.

Amongst liberi homines, liberi homines tenentes, or
liberi homines sub regis, in every English shire, the
Domesday Book records the names of *Freewomen*.

I have personally searched the Records of Stratford-
upon-Avon. There women could be burgesses. One
entry, noted for another purpose, I may here quote:
"At a Hall holden in the Gildehall, 9th September,
1573, Adrian Queeney and John Shakespeare being
present, the town council received . . . of Christian White

for her sisterhood, 6s. 8d. ; Robert Wright for his brotherhood, 6s. 8d."

York. "Women being free of the city, on marrying a man who is not free, forfeit their freedom. Persons are entitled to become free by birth, by apprenticeship, or by gift or grant. Every person who has served an apprenticeship for seven years under a binding by indentures for that period to a freeman or freewoman inhabiting and carrying on trade in the city is entitled to become free. The indentures may be assigned to another master or mistress being free. The privileges of freemen are extended to the partners of freemen and to their widows." ("Report of Municipal Corporation Committee, 1835," p. 1741.)

The customs of Doncaster seem somewhat similar. (*See* same report, p. 1497.)

The City of Chester followed the custom of London. (*See* "The Mayor's Book of Chester, 1597-8.")

Letter from Lord Burleigh to the officers of the Port of Chester, authorising them to enter without tax the Gascony wines of a city merchant's widow :—

"After my hartie commendacions, Whereas I understand that you have made scruple to take entrie of certeine Tonnes of Gascoigne wynes brought into that port in december laste, being the proper goodes of Ales Massy, wydowe, late wife of William Massy, merchant, of that cittie, deceased, as also of certeine other Tonnes of Gascoign wynes, brought in thither by William Massey, his sonne, late merchant and free citesin of that cittie, also deceased, whose administratrix the said Ales Massy is. For-as-much as I fynde by a graunte by privy seale, from hir Majestie, dated the 21st daye of Maye, in the ninth yere of hir raigne, that her pleasure is (for good consideracion in the said pryvye seale specified) That all merchants, inhabitants, and Free Citizens of that Cittie shal be freed and discharged from payment of any Imposte for such wynes as they bring into that port. And forasmuch as also I have receyved a Lettre from the Maior and Aldermen of that cittie, whereby they doe certifye unto me that all Freemen's wydowes of that cittie, during their wydowehood, by the Custom of the said Cittie, have used, and ought to have and enioie all such Trades, Fredomes and Liberties as their husbandes used in their life tyme, which custome hath bene used and allowed of tyme out of mynde. Therefore, these are to will and require you to take entrie of all the aforesaid wynes of the said Wydow Massies as well those that she hath as administratrix to Wm. Massey, as of hir owne proper wynes, without taking or demaundinge Impost for the same wynes. And this shal be your discharge in that behalf. From my house at Westminster, the xiiith of April, 1598.

"Your lovinge frende,

"W. BURGHLEY.

"To my loving frendes, ye Officers of ye Port of Chester."

" Recepta per nos viii. die Maii per manus Richardi Massy.   "THO. FLETCHER, Maior."*

In 1597, by the same books, some money was distributed to twenty poor people, having been free of the city twenty years at least; among these were five women.

In the Town of Winchester women could be free.   In an old Customary of that town we may find "Every woman selling Bread in the High Street, not having the freedom, pays to the King 2s. 5d. a year, and to the City Clerk 1d., if she sells by the year, if less, in proportion.   Every woman who brews for sale is to make good beer.   No Brewer not free of the City (nul Brasceresse hors de Franchise) can brew within the City jurisdiction without compounding with the Bailiff." (*Archæological Journal*, vol. iv., 1852.)

In the Hall-book of the Corporation of Leicester 1621, we find :

"It is agreed by a generall consent that Wm. Hartshorne, husbandman, shall be made ffreeman of corporacon payinge such ffine as Mr. Maiour and the Chambleyns that now be shall assess.   But he is not allowed any freedom or privilege by reason that his mother was a ffreewoman.   Neither is it thought fit that any woman be hereafter made free of this corporacon." ("Notes and Queries," vol. v., 5th series, p. 138.)

This note is important as showing the period of the change of tone and spirit.

* Transcribed by Dr. Furnival for his work on the Chester MSS.

Women could be on the Corporation.—In 1593, in the
Archives of the Borough of Maidstone, Kent, appears,
" That the 11th of September, 1593, Rose Cloke, single
woman (according to the order and constitutions of the
town and parish of Maidstone aforesaid), was admitted
to be one of the corporation and body politique of the
same town and parish, from henceforth to enjoy the
liberties and franchises of the same in every respect, as
others the freemen of the said town and parish.   And
she was also then sworn accordingly, and for some
reasonable causes and considerations then stated she
was released from paying any fine, other than for her
said oath, which she then paid accordingly " (" Notes and
Queries," vol. xii., 5th series, 318).   The transcriber
doubts the " legality " of Miss Rose Cloke's election.
But it was not till a very long time after this date that
any attempt was made to interfere with the liberty of
the electors in choosing whom they would.

Queen Elizabeth is said to have reproached the
women of Kent for not more fully exercising their
privileges.   It may have been in connection with this
illustration as to what their privileges might be.   I had
long meditated on the inner meaning of this reproach,
before I came upon the elucidation.   She was a Kentish
woman herself, having been born in Greenwich.   The
freemen of Kent alone, in England, rose in arms against
William the Conqueror, and would not lay them down
until their ancient laws and customs were confirmed to
them.   " All the bodies of Kentish men are free."   The

Custumal of Kent, based on the ancient Saxon laws, gave wider privilege to women than the Normanised laws of the rest of the country. Inheritance was originally equal and independent of sex, either in relations of descent or of marriage. The children all inherited equally, with a certain special tender consideration for the *youngest*, male or female.

I know that by later developments the Custumal of Kent in regard to inheritance became gradually assimilated to that of the rest of England. But if we refer to Wilkins' "Laws of the Anglo-Saxons," p. 225, we shall find that William the Conqueror granted to the people the laws which had been used in England. The Clause on Intestates runs: "If a man die intestate, his children, 'liberi' (not filii or pueri in Latin), les enfans (not fils in Norman-French), equally divide his property among them." Henry I. confirmed this (*see* p. 234).

Selden, speaking of Tacitus, says ("Janus Anglorum," c. 21): "Everyone's children are their heirs and successors, and there was no will"; and speaking for himself, he says: "Anciently, if I be not mistaken, most inheritances were parted among the *children*." It is interesting to compare the later editions of Hallam's "History of the Middle Ages" with his earlier ones. He gradually found out that the estates were not restricted to males, even in "Leg. Salicæ, c. 62," among the Burgundians, the Visigoths, the French. The laws of Canute (68) rule that a man's property

should be distributed between his wife and children
(*liberis*, not *pueris*). "It was the opinion of Lord
Holt, in the case of Blackborough *v.* Davis (Salk.
251, S.C. 1 Peere Wil. 50), that by the Common Law,
both before and at the Conquest, all the children, male
and female, inherited as well the real as the personal
estate of the ancestor equally and in like proportion."
(*See* Robinson's Law Dictionary, p. 9.) "Ordinary
lands, at least, descended to *all* the children." (Hale's
Hist. Com. Law, 219; Parker's Ant. Ed. Brit., 108;
C. J. Holt, in Clement *v.* Scudamore, 6 Mod. Rep.,
121.) By the reign of Henry II. there began to be a
preference for males. The Custumal of Kent, as given
in the time of Edward II., states that all the sons
inherit before all the daughters. Primogeniture was
introduced in 31 Hen. VIII., c. 3, to Kent; and 34
and 35 Hen. VIII., c. 26, to Wales; in 23 Eliz. 17,
to Exeter; but it was optional whether to choose the
new or the old principle of inheritance. In gavelkind
lands, if a father had sons, and one of them died in
his lifetime, leaving a daughter, she inherited with
her uncles, for she is the daughter of a male, *jure
representationis* (1 Salk. 243). (*See* also Sommer on
gavelkind.)

A widow had the half of her husband's property
till she married again; a widower had the half of his
wife's property *while he remained single*. In the Rot.
Hundredorum and Testa de Nevil, the large proportion of women landowners show how it worked

out. This comparative equality in property necessarily gave the women of Kent fuller privilege. The recognition of the freedom of womanhood naturally made the men of Kent more free. "Of all the English shires, be thou surnamed the Free." (Drayton's "Poly-Olbion, Song 18th.")

Yet some of the English shires did not lag far behind Kent. "By the custom of Borough English, the widow shall have the *whole* of her husband's lands in dower, which is called her *free-bench;* and this is given to her, the better to provide for the younger children, with the care of whom she is entrusted. (Co. Litt. 111; F. N. B., 150, Tomlin's Law Dictionary.)

We may cite "A customary or note of such customes as hath bin used, time out of mind, in Aston and Coat in ye parish of Bampton in ye county of Oxon, and is att this time used and kept as appeareth by ye *sixteens* who hath hereunto, with ye consent of ye inhabitants of ye said Aston and Coat, sett their hands and seals the sixt September, in ye 35th yeare of Queen Elizabeth, Anno Dom. 1593." The "customary" contains twelve articles regulating the election and duties of the sixteens, of which the first is : "The Custome is that upon our Lady-day Eve every yeere, all the *Inhabitants* of Aston and Coat shall meet at Aston Crosse about three of ye clock in ye afternoone, or one of everye House to understand who shall serve for ye sixteen for that year coming, and to choose other officers for ye same yeere. (2) Ye said

H

sixteens being known, ye hundred tenants of ye same sixteens doe divide themselves some distance from ye Lords Tenants of ye said sixteens. And ye Hundreds Tenants do chuse one Grasse Steward and one Water Hayward, and the Lords Tennants do choose two Grasse Stewards and one Water Hayward, etc. This antient custome have ben confirmed in ye 35th yeare of Queen Elizabeth, 1593, by most of ye substantiall inhabitants of Aston and Coat, videl:

"Roger Medhop (gent).
The mark of Richard Stacy.
The mark of Eliz. Alder.
The mark of John Humphries.
The mark of Margery Young.
The mark of John Bricklande.
The mark of Will. Young.
The mark of Thos. Walter.
The mark of Will. Wagh.
The mark of John Newman.
The mark of Richard Thynne.
The mark of Robt. Carter.
The mark of Will. Haukes.
The mark of Ann Startupp.
The mark of Will Tisbee.
The mark of John Pryor.
The mark of John Church."

(*Archæologia*, vol. xxxv., p. 472), which adds: "Similar customs were formerly practised in Sussex, and may be found in the Sussex Archæological Collections."

We find another case in Grant's " Treatise of the Law of Corporations," p. 6.

"In general women cannot be corporators, although in some hospitals they may be so, and there is one instance in the books of a Corporation consisting of Brethren and Sisters, and invested with municipal powers to a certain extent, in The Pontenarii of Maidenhead (*vide* Rep. 30). (Palmer's "Cases," p. 77, 17 Jac., B.R.) " Quo Warranto vers Corporation de Maydenhead en Berkshire, pur claymer de certaine Franchises et Liberties, un Market, chescun Lundie, Pickage, Stallage, Toll, etc." (Rot. Cor. 106.) They pleaded that the Bridge had been repaired by a Fraternitie, time out of mind, which was dissolved, and that the King by Letters Patent, on condition that they repaired the Bridge, granted them a market every Monday with all Liberties. . . . " Et le veritie fuit que Hen. 6, ad incorporate un Corporation la *per nomen Gardianorum Fratrum et Sororum Pontenariorum et concessit* al eux et lour Successors *quod ipsi et Successores sui haberent mercatum quolibet die lunae prout ante habuissent simul cum Tolneto, Pickagio, Stallagio, etc.*" The opinion of three Judges was "que Toll fuit bien grant non obstant que le quantitie de Argent d'estre payé pur Toll pur chescun chose ne fuit expresse, Mes Montague Ch. Justice fuit cont, Mes que le Corporation enjoyera les Privileges non obstant cest action port." In page 626 of Grant's Treatise, we see " A Corporation Sole is a Body Politic having perpetual succession, and being

constituted in a single person. . . . Corporations Sole
are chiefly Ecclesiastical, one or two instances only of
Lay Corporations Sole occurring in the Books. . . . The
most important Corporation of this nature that claims
attention is the King. . . . It is as a Body Corporate
that the King is said to be immortal (Howell's "State
Trials," 598). . . . A Queen Regnant is precisely and
in the same way and to all intents a Corporation, and,
indeed, there is nothing inconsistent with the principles
of the old Law in this; it was every day's experience
before the Reformation to find female subjects as
Corporations Sole, as Lady Abbesses, etc., but since
that era it is superfluous to observe, females cannot be
invested with this description of incorporation, though,
as we have seen, they may be Corporators of Hospitals,
Railways, and other trading bodies." (Note. *See*
"Abbess of Brinham's Case." Year-book, Ed. III.,
vol. xxiii.; 2 Rolle's Abr. 348, l. 33; and Colt &
Glover *v.* Bishop of Coventry, Hob. 148, 149.)

They could vote for Members of Parliament. — To
their Municipal Rights were added, in the reign of
Henry III., their Parliamentary Rights.

In 25 Edward I., The Statute De tallagio non concedendo, declared that "no tallage or aid shall be levied
by us, or by our heirs in the realm, without the goodwill
and assent of . . . Knights, Burgesses, and other
Freemen of the Land." * (*See* 1 Steph. Com. 165,
note, 12th edition.)

* Hallam's "Middle Ages," p. 557, Note 3.

As women were Burgesses and Liberi Homines, the right was *given* to them as well as to men. Plowden ("Jura Anglorum," p. 438) remarks that "the Knights of the Shire represented landed property, the Burgesses the interests of manufacture or trade"; as women could be Traders they were recognised as having the rights of Traders.

The qualifications of Electors in Boroughs were very far from uniform or certain, as may have been noted in the Gatton case.

In Bath the Franchise was limited to the Mayor and Corporation. Sometimes it was limited to freeholders, sometimes to freeholders resident, at other times to inhabitants, in other cases to inhabitants paying Scot and Lot.

In London the Franchise was exercised by all paying Scot or Lot.

In Newcastle-on-Tyne, the Franchise naturally devolved on a Freeman's widow, who could also carry on his business. (Brand's "History and Antiquities of Newcastle," vol. ii., p. 367.)

The ordinances of Worcester (6 Edward IV., 49)—"Also that every eleccion of citizens for to come to the Parliament, that they be chosen openly in the gelde Halle of such as ben dwellynge within the fraunches and by the moste voice, according to the lawe and to the statutes in such cases ordayned and not privily" ("Early English Gilds," J. Toulmin Smith).

In Shrewsbury, prior to the Reform Act, the right of

returning members of Parliament for the Borough was
vested exclusively in *Burgesses* paying Scot and Lot.
("Mun. Corp. Com.," p. 2014.)

Rhuddlan — " Here, as in the other contributory
Boroughs to Flint, the franchise is exercised by all
resident inhabitants paying Scot and Lot." (" Mun.
Corp. Com.," p. 2840.)

In the Reports of Controverted Elections, Luders
mentions that of Lyme Regis, 1789. The dispute was
whether non-resident burgesses could record their vote.
Among the old burgess lists brought forward to elucidate
the qualifications for electors, that of 29th September, 19
Eliz., was produced. The first three names on the list
were of three women—" Burgenses sive liberi tenentes
Elizabetha filia Thomæ Hyatt, Crispina Bowden Vidua,
Alicia Toller Vidua," then follow the names of several
men. To these were added in 21 Eliz. two names of
" liberi burgenses jure uxoris." Later records show an
increased number of women's names on the register of
this borough.

The case of Holt *v.* Lyle, or Coates *v.* Lisle in 4
James I., in discussing the right of a clergyman to vote,
affirms as a side issue that "a *feme sole,* if she have a
freehold, can vote for a Parliament man, but if she is
married, her husband must vote for her." (*Cited* by
C. J. Lee in Olive *v.* Ingram, 7 Modern Reports, 271.)
A limitation again expressed in Catharine *v.* Surry,
preserved in Hakewell's " Manuscript Cases."

As some have attempted to throw doubts on the

authenticity of these cases, quoted as they were by
the Lord Chief-Justice from the Bench in 1739, it
may be well to note here that "William Hakewell was
a great student of legal antiquities, and a Master of
Precedents" ("Dictionary of National Biography").
He left Parliamentary life in 1629, the year after he
had, in the Committee of Parliamentary Privileges,
helped to decide on the Gatton case. He was one
of the six lawyers appointed to revise the Laws, and
was thereafter created Master of Chancery. So one
might be tempted to consider him rather an exception-
ally good and trustworthy witness. He helped to
decide other points in connection with the Franchise,
which it is important for us to remember. He not
only decided that inhabitant suffrage must supersede
freeholding, that taxation gave the right to representation, but that, from its very nature, no desuetude could
take away the right of voting. "On 9th April, 1614,
it was pleaded, Sithence Durham last drawn into
charge to join in petition to the King that Durham
may have writs for Knights and Burgesses. Said to
be dumb men because no voices. Mr. Ashley said,
They of Durham had held it a privilege not to be
bound to attendance to Parliament. On 31st May
was read An Act for Knights and Burgesses to have
places in Parliament, for the County Palatine, City
of Durham and the Borough of Castle Barnard." "On
14th March, 1620, members were allowed for the
Palatinate of Durham, which had hitherto sat free from

taxation, and consequently sent no members to the House of Commons. It was allowed without discussion by the House," taxation and representation being constitutionally inseparable. (*See Commons' Journal*, 14th March, 1620.)

"Regarding towns that had discontinued long sending of any burgesses, and yet were allowed." Hakewell had discovered this of " Millborne Port, County Somerset, and Webly, County Hereford, that, either from poverty or ignorance of their right, or neglect of the Sheriff, had ceased voting. After 321 years they elected again." "In 21 Jac. I. also, Amersham, Wendover, Great Marlowe, in Buckinghamshire, were in the same condition, but received writs for return upon application." (*See* Addit. MS., Brit. Mus. 8980.) Thus the doctrine that the right to the Franchise never lapses, and that *non-user* never deprives an Elector of this privilege, was affirmed by the Committee of Privileges in the Parliament of which Coke and Hakewell were members.

CHAPTER VII

THE LONG EBB

"Ye have made the law of none effect by your tradition."

The Errors of Sir Edward Coke.—In a historical treatise it is not necessary fully to analyse causes. Facts must be left to speak for themselves. It is a patent fact that, early in the seventeenth century, men's views regarding women became much altered, and the liberties of women thereby curtailed. But there is generally one voice that in expressing seems to lead the opinion of an age. The accepted voice of this period, on this subject, was not that of the "learned Selden"* but of the "illegal Coke."

* "Mr. Selden, who is well known to have the learning of 20 men, and the honesty of as many." (History of Magna Charta, p. 95.) Selden writes warmly in favour of women, and quotes many authorities in support of his opinion. Besides those that have been quoted, we may notice that he refers to Sir Thomas More's Utopia. "Plato allowed women to govern, nor did Aristotle (whatever the Interpreters of his Politics foolishly say) take from them that privilege. Virtue shuts no door against anybody, any sex, but freely admits all. And Hermes Trismegistus, that thrice great man, in his Poemander, according to his knowledge of Heavenly concerns (and that sure was great in comparison of what the owl-eyed Philosophers had) he ascribes the mystical name of MALE-FEMALE to the great Understanding, to wit, God the Governor of the Universe." ("Janus Anglorum," chap. xii.)

He first pronounced an opinion on the disability of women, and, as every other *so-called authority* depends upon his, it is necessary to examine the grounds of his opinion first, as with him all his followers must stand or fall.

When he was speaking against the Procuratores Cleri (Proctors of the Clergy) having a voice in Parliament, it was urged on him that it was unjust that persons should have to be bound by laws which they had had no voice in making. To this he replied : " In many cases multitudes are bound by Acts of Parliament which are not parties to the elections of knights, citizens and burgesses, as all they that have no freehold, or have freehold in ancient demesne ; and *all women having freehold or no freehold*, and men within the age of one-and-twenty years " (" Fourth Institute," 5). He quotes no record, he suggests no authority, he adduces no precedent. He could not. Yet from this one *obiter dictum* of his, uttered in the heat of his discussion against clergymen, recorded in loose notes, and published without correction after his death, has arisen all consequent opinion, custom and *law* against the Woman's Franchise. So terrible can be the consequences of the by-utterances of a Judge when *careless, prejudiced, or wilfully ignorant.* That Coke could be all three it is easy to prove.

(1) In regard to the suspicions attending the death of Prince Henry, Sir Anthony Weldon records—" It was intended the Law should run in its proper channel, but was stopt, and put out of its course by the folly of that

great Clerke, though no wise man, Sir Edward Coke." (*See* the Court and Character of King James.)

In Prynne's " Introduction to the Animadversions on the Fourth Part of the Lawe of England," he says : " My ardent desires and studious endeavours to benefit the present age and posterity to my power by advancing learning . . . by discovering sundry misquotations, mistakes of records in our printed law-books' reports, especially in the Institute of that eminent pillar of the Common Law, Sir Edward Coke, published with some disadvantage to him and his readers since his death, whose quotations (through too much credulity and supineness) are generally received, relied on, by a mere implicit faith, as infallible Oracles, without the least examination of their originals."

Male credulity in regard to Coke has been the cause of so much direct and indirect suffering to women that it is not surprising that they now attempt to get behind "the Oracle," and question the Spirit itself of the English Constitution. Many other writers besides Prynne refer to Coke's want of care. The Lord Coke in his preface to Littleton, thinks Littleton's " Tenures " were first printed in 24 Henry VIII. ; my Lord was mistaken. (J. C. Anstiss Nicholl's, " Illustrations of Literature.") " In 1615 the King told him to take into consideration and review his Book of Reports ; wherein, as His Majesty is informed, be many extravagant and exorbitant opinions set down and published for positive and good law." (Chalmers' Biog. Dict.) " The

Institutes published in his lifetime were very incorrect. The 4th part not being published till after his death, there are many and greater inaccuracies in it." One example in the contested passage may be noted. He says that those who had no freehold had no vote. He did not die until 1634, and the notes for the "Fourth Institute" were the last work of his life. But J. Glanville's "Reports of Election Cases," 21 and 22 James I., prove that by the Parliaments of 1621 and 1628 the Franchise was declared to be vested in *inhabitant householders whether freeholders or not*, so Coke was incorrect as to that statement at least.

(2) That, through prejudice, he could be blinded to Justice can be seen in that picture preserved by his Biographers of his hounding Sir Walter Raleigh to his death by virulent unjudicial denunciations; or in that other when he and his followers made a riot with swords and staves in seizing his daughter from the home in which his wife (formerly Lady Hatton) had placed her. The King's Council severely reprimanded him for his illegal action then. (*See* "The Letter of the Council to Sir Thomas Lake regarding the Proceedings of Sir Edward Coke at Oatlands," "Camden Miscell.," vol. v.)

The petition of Sir Francis Michell to the House of Commons, 23rd February, 1620, contains trenchant criticisms on Coke's conduct as partial and passionate. Though they may be somewhat discounted by the writer's position, they must have had some basis of truth. Michell said that when summoned before the Bar, Sir Edward Coke prejudiced his cause by saying aloud, " When I was Chief-Justice, I knew Sir Francis Michell; he is a *tainted man*," which saying discouraged his friends from speaking on his behalf. He repeats elsewhere that Coke was wont " to make invectives by the hour-glass "; and indeed adds many other more serious charges. Michell was put out, as was the custom, when his case was being discussed. In his absence he˙ was condemned to go to the Tower, and on being readmitted, thought he was to be allowed to defend himself, as was the custom, and "asked leave to speak for himself, which Sir Edward Coke *hastened to refuse*" (Sir Simon d'Ewes' Papers, Harl. MSS., 158, f. 224). " His rancour, descending to Brutality was infamous " (Dict. Nat. Biog.). Sir Francis Bacon writes to him : " As your pleadings were wont to insult our misery and inveigh literally against the person, so are you still careless in this point to praise or dispraise upon slight grounds and that suddenly, so that your reproofs or commendations are for the most part neglected and contemned, when the censure of a Judge coming slow but sure should be a brand to the guilty and a crown to the virtuous. . . . You make the laws too much lean to your opinion, whereby you show yourself to be a legal tyrant." Foss in his " Lives of the Judges," vi. 12, says: " In the trial of Essex, he gave the first specimen of that objurgatory and coarse style which makes his oratory so painfully remembered." Later, speaking of the trials for the murder of Sir Thomas Averbury, Foss says: "Guilty as the parties undoubtedly were, Coke conducted the trial most unfairly." James I. is known to have called him "the fittest engine for a tyrant ever was in England."

Sir Edward Conway writes of him in 1624: "Sir Edward Coke would die if he could not help to ruin a great man once in seven years."

He was an only son with seven sisters, which position probably made him overvalue his own sex. His well-known matrimonial disputes probably helped to increase his prejudice against the other sex.

(3) That he could be *wilfully ignorant* there is abundant ground to believe. He married again five months after his first wife's death, without Banns or License, and to escape Excommunication, he pleaded Ignorance of the Law! "Not only does he interpolate, but he is often inaccurate; sometimes, as in Gage's case, he gives a wrong account of the decision, and still more often the authorities he cites do not bear out his propositions of law. This is a fault common to his Reports and his Institutes alike, and it has had very serious consequences upon English Law" (Dict. Nat. Biog.). Holt *v.* Lyle, or Coates *v.* Lisle and Catharine *v.* Surry, *cited* in Olive *v.* Ingram (7 Mod. Rep., 263), had been decided when he was Attorney-General. These affirmed that "a *feme sole* could vote for a Parliament man."

The Gatton case had been decided in a Parliament, and by a Committee of which he was a member; and whether he had concurred in it or not, he cannot but have been aware that other members of Parliament, even in his day, allowed the woman's privilege.

Others have accused him of suppressing and falsifying legal documents. (*See* Chisholm Anstey's "Supposed Constitutional Restraints.") Chief-Justice Best from the Bench said, " I am afraid that we should get rid of a good deal of what is considered law in Westminster Hall if what Lord Coke says *without authority* is not law." (2 C. P. Bingham's Law Reports, 296, Garland *v.* Jekyll.)

One other case which afterwards told heavily upon women we may note. " Coke artfully inserted in the marriage settlement of his fourth son John, with the daughter and heiress of Anthony Wheatley, a clause of reversion to *his own heirs* to the exclusion of heirs female, which was not discovered until 1671, when John having died, leaving seven daughters, their mother's paternal inheritance passed away from them to their uncle Robert, Coke's fifth son."

" His legal propositions may often be unsound in substance, but in his mode of stating what he believes or wishes to be law, he often reaches the perfection of form " (Dict. Nat. Biography). This "*form*" may be sufficient to satisfy legal technicalities, but I think I have brought forward enough to show that intelligent women have reason to object to him as a "tainted " authority.

Coke tells us in his "Fourth Institute" what properties a Parliament man should have. "He should have three properties of the elephant; first, that he hath no gall; second, that he is inflexible and cannot bow; third, that he is of a most ripe and perfect memory. First to be without gall—that is, without malice, rancour, hate and envy." We have shown that Coke was deficient in the first quality prescribed by himself for just judgment. His abject submission to the Archbishop after his Breach of the Canon Law, shows that he could bow very low to escape the consequences of his wrong - doing; his grovelling in the dust before James, when he had roused the King to wrath, shows that he could do the same when he thought he was right, "from which we may learn that he was, as such men always are, as dejected and fawning in adversity as he was insolent and over-bearing in prosperity" (Chalmers' "Dict. Biog."). We must now prove that he was deficient in the third quality also. His memory was imperfect. He forgot one Statute when he was criticising another; he forgot what he had written in the "Second Institute," when he was preparing his manuscript for the Fourth. It is only by self-contradiction that he can hold the opinion now under discussion. From his own works we must judge him on this count (Coke *v.* Coke). In the "Fourth Institute," 5, he classifies women with minors. In the "Second Institute," c. iii., 96, his authorised and corrected work, he says, on the contrary : "Seeing that a *feme sole* that cannot perform knight's service may serve by deputy, it may be demanded wherefore an heir male, being within the age of twenty-one years, may not likewise serve by deputy. To this it is answered, that in cases of minoritie all is one to both sexes, viz., if the heire male be at the death of the ancestor under the age of one-and-twenty years, or the heire female under the age of fourteen, they can make no deputy, but the Lord will have wardship. Therefore, Littleton is here to be understood of a *feme sole* of full age and seized of land, holden by knight's service,* either by purchase or descent." One would have thought this clear enough for a legal mind to follow. Women do not, therefore, come into the same class as minors in regard to their appointing deputies. But they do come into the class of Electors. ("Second Institute," 119.) "A woman may be a free suitor to the Courts of the Lord, and though it be generally said that the free Suitors be Judges in these courts, this is intended of men and not of women."

I have already noted the illegal character of this opinion; but I repeat it here intentionally. Coke does not see that in avoiding one of the horns of a dilemma he throws himself on the other. If "women could be suitors," and were "not intended to be judges" or pares, the only other duty left them as suitors would be "to elect their knights of the shire!"

* In discussing the " Parliament of Marlebridge " (52 Henry III., c. vi., p. 3) he says: "Albeit the heir be not *primogenitus*, but an heir female, or male, lineal or collateral, yet everyone of them be within the same mischief."

I

The study of the original statutes supports the freedom
of women as to both duties, as well as the fact of their
having exercised that freedom.   In Howell's "State
Trials," xix. (Entick *v.* Carrington, 6 George III.), there
is a question asked and answered, worthy of repetition
here — Lord Chief-Justice Camden said (at p. 1071):
"Can the Judges extrajudicially make a thing law to bind
the Kingdom by a declaration that such is their opinion?
I say no.   It is a matter of impeachment for any judge
to affirm it.   There must be an antecedent principle
or authority from whence this opinion may be fairly
collected, otherwise the opinion is null, and nothing
but ignorance can excuse the judge that subscribed
it."   That women had to submit then is no reason
that they should submit now, as the same case explains
—"It would be strange doctrine to assert that all the
people of this land were bound to acknowledge that as
universal law which a few had been afraid to dispute."
Butler notices that Coke had not studied the Feudal
Law (Dict. Nat. Biog.)   This may partially account for
his ignorance concerning women, whose relations to
representation he evidently had not studied   He
who drew up the famous "Petition of Rights" for
men has, by his careless or premeditated words, been
the means of a *denial of rights* to women.

A believer in Coke's views and methods of per-
petuating them was Sir Simon d'Ewes, High Sheriff of
Suffolk. At the elections of 1640 (19th and 22nd October)
Sir Roger North and his Royalist friends had charged

him with partiality towards the Puritan candidates. He cleared himself eagerly and then added : " It is true that by the ignorance of some of the Clarkes at the other two tables, the **oaths of some single women that were freeholders** were taken without the knowledge of the said High Sheriff, who as soone as he had notice thereof instantly sent to forbidd the same, conceiving it a matter verie unworthie of any gentleman, and most dishonorable in such an election, to make use of their voices, *although in law they might have been allowed.* Nor did the High Sheriff allow of the said votes, upon his numbering of the said Poll, but with the allowance and consent of the said two Knights themselves, discount them and cast them out " (Sir Simon d'Ewes' Papers ; Harl. MS., 158). Thus in a second illustrative case, personal opinion and prejudice were allowed to counteract law and privilege. And the law-abiding women yielded to what they were told was law, and, being kept in ignorance, they knew no better.

But in the very next year women showed that they took a strong interest in public affairs.

In vol. ii., p. 1673, Parliamentary History, is preserved the Petition to the Commons for Redress of Grievances, 4th February, 1641. On the last day of sitting many women had been observed to crowd much about the door of the Commons, and Sergeant-Major Skippon applied to the House to know what to do with them, they telling him that where there was one now there would be 500 next day. The House bade him speak them fair.

Next day they presented their petition (printed by John Wright at King's Head in Old Bailey).

"To the Honourable Knights, Citizens, and Burgesses of the House of Commons assembled in Parliament, the Humble Petition of the Gentlewomen, Tradesmen's Wives, and many others of the Female Sex, all inhabitants of London and the Suburbs thereof, with the lowest submission showing, etc."

They acknowledge the care of the House in the affairs of State. They have cheerfully joined in petitions which have been exhibited "in behalf of the purity of religion and the liberty of our husbands' persons and estates." "We counting ourselves to have an interest in the common privileges with them."

"It may be thought strange and unbeseeming to our sex to show ourselves by way of petition to this Honourable Assembly. But the matter being rightly considered of . . . it will be found a duty commanded and required. (1) Because Christ hath purchased us at as dear a rate as he hath done men, and therefore requireth like obedience for the same mercy as men. (2) Because in the free enjoying of Christ in His own laws, and a flourishing estate of the Church and Commonwealth consisteth the happiness of women as well as of men. (3) Because women are sharers in the common calamities that accompany both Church and Commonwealth, when oppression is exercised over the Church or Kingdom wherein they live; and unlimited power given to the prelates to exercise authority over the consciences of women as well as men : witness Newgate and Smithfield, and other places of persecution, wherein women, as well as men, have felt the smart of their fury," etc.

"The petition was presented by Mrs. Anne Stagg, a gentlewoman and brewer's wife, and many others with her of like rank and quality. Mr. Pym came to the Commons' door, addressed the women and told them that their petition had been thankfully accepted and would be carefully considered."

Coke's papers had been seized by the King at his death in 1634, but on the 12th May, 1641, the House of Commons ordered Coke's heir to print them, and thus his views on this point were perpetuated.

On the 13th February, 1620, Coke had committed the House to extraordinary doctrine in another relation to women. Among Mr. Lovell's witnesses was a lady, Mrs. Newdigate, "the House calling to have them called in. Sir Edward Coke out of St. Barnard said, A woman ought not to speak in the congregation. Examination hereof committed to a committee" (*Commons' Journal*). It is strange that Sir Edward Coke should have gone so far afield as St. Barnard when St. Paul might have come in as conveniently. Had he read the Gospels as carefully as he had read St. Barnard, he would have seen that one of the first two preachers of Christ was Anna the prophetess, who spake of Him in the temple to all them that looked for redemption in Jerusalem (Luke ii. 36), and that it was through women that Christ sent the first message to the Apostles and

Disciples, that became the watchword of early Chris-
tianity, "Christ is arisen" (Matthew xxviii., Luke xxiv.,
John xx.).   Coke's precedent on this point was reversed
in his own century.

On the 17th November, 1666, "Some debate arising
whether Mrs. Bodville, mother of Mrs. Roberts, should
be admitted as witness, the matter being debated in the
House, the question being put whether Mrs. Bodville be
admitted, it was resolved in the affirmative, and Mrs.
Bodville, with several other witnesses, was examined"
(*Commons' Journal*).

His utterance on the Women's Franchise has coloured
the minds of willing disciples until to-day.   In Add.
MS., British Museum, 25, 271, Hakewell on impositions,
says : "To make a man judge in his own cause, and
especiallie ye mightie over ye weake, and that in pointe
of profitt to him that judgeth, were to leave a way
open to oppression and bondage."   So women proved.
There is no doubt that Puritanism on the one hand,
and the frivolity of the fashions of the Restoration on
the other, tended to make women content with their
narrowed political privileges, and restricted educational
opportunities.   Only among the Society of Friends,
commonly called Quakers, did women retain their
natural place.   Though there were some brilliant
exceptions, the majority of women, by the procrustean
methods of treatment in vogue were reduced to the
state of incompetency that society came to believe was
natural to them.   "It was unwomanly for women to

think and act for themselves." "Women had no concern in public affairs." "Men knew much better than women did what was good for them," were proverbs.

By losing one privilege they lost others. New laws were made prejudicial to their interests, and old laws retranslated in a new and narrow spirit. Precedent gained power to override statute; the notions of justice between the sexes became warped and distorted.

The rules of inheritance were altered, the rights of women in their property further ignored. Sophistical Labour Creeds were introduced to support masculine property privilege. Work came to be considered ignoble for *ladies*, except when done without remuneration; domestic work was not cognisable in coin of the realm, therefore women were said to be *supported* by their male relatives, though they might labour ten times as much as they. It was natural to educate them little, so that they should not know; it was natural to take privileges from those who knew not what they lost.

Protesting Women.—But the Suppression of the Sex did not go on without various Protests on the part of women during the 200 years of this Backdraw in the tide of Civilisation. We cannot spare time for every detail; but three illustrative women must be noted— the first, born in the sixteenth century, protesting against the infringement of the Inheritance Laws in relation to women; the second, born in the seventeenth century, against the withdrawal of their educational advantages;

the third, born in the eighteenth century, against their social, civil and political degradation.

Anne Clifford, born in 1590, was the only daughter of George, Earl of Cumberland, and of his goodwife, Margaret Russell. She and her two noble sisters, Elizabeth, Countess of Bath, and Anne, Countess of Warwick, were distinguished for family affection, and all other womanly virtues. The Countess of Warwick was Elizabeth's favourite Lady-in-Waiting. Anne was much with this aunt in her youth, was a favourite of Queen Elizabeth, and was destined for her Court. Her father refused to allow her, like other noble ladies of her time, to learn ancient and modern languages, so she made the most of the opportunities to be found in her own. " Her instructor in her younger years was the learned Mr. Daniel, the Historiographer and Poet. She was much interested in searching out old documents about her ancestors and very jealous of preserving her rights." (*See* in Nicolson and Burn's " History of Westmoreland and Cumberland," the Autobiography of Mr. Sedgwick, who was her Secretary.) She was well prepared by her beloved mother and respected tutor for the exigencies of her future life. The Queen died in 1602-3, and her father in 1605. A woman being considered of age at fourteen, she chose her mother as her guardian, who initiated the proceedings against her brother-in-law, the new Earl of Cumberland, which lasted until his death. The Earldom of Cumberland had been entailed in Heirs Male, but the secondary Titles, the Baronies of Clifford, Westmoreland,

and Vescy, with all the Lands and Castles in West-moreland belonging to them, were entailed in the Heir General. Her uncle, however, took possession, and favoured by the King, the power of wealth, and Sex Bias among those in power, he was able to hold them against her, in spite of her private and public petitions. His son, Henry, was summoned to Parliament by the title of Lord Clifford, a right which should have been hers, as she bitterly complained. Meanwhile, in 1609, she married Richard, Earl of Dorset. " On 25th July, 1610, my cousin, Henry, married Lady Francis Cecil, daughter to Robert, Earl Salisbury, which marriage was purposely made that by that power and greatness of his the lands of mine inheritance might be worsted and kept by strong hand from me " (Harl. MS., 6177, Anne Clifford's Diary). 16th July, 1615, "the great trial for my lands in Craven." Her husband agreed with the Earl of Cumberland to leave it to the King's arbitration, which she would never agree to, standing upon her rights. In 1617 she was brought before King James in Whitehall to give her consent to the arbitration, " which I utterly refused, and was thereby afterwards brought to many and great troubles." Her uncle offered £20,000 as a compromise for the Westmoreland estates, which she would not hear of, but which her prodigal husband urged her to accept. Indeed, he attempted to strain his marital rights, and backed by the King, signed the agreement with her uncle, which she refused to acknow-ledge, and defeated the plans of the trio by her firmness.

For she was a true descendant of the old stock of women, and wished "to live and die with the feeling that she is receiving what she must hand down to her children neither tarnished nor depreciated, what future daughters-in-law may receive, and so pass on to her grandchildren" (Tac. Germ., c. 18). She was determined to hold by her rightful inheritance. Her husband died on 28th March, 1624, and the contest went on with renewed vigour.

In the Domestic Series, "State Papers," vol. cxxvi., 7, 1628, there is preserved "Reasons to prove that by the Common Law dignities conferred by Writ of Summons to Parliament descend to females, where there is a sole heir, and not co-heirs; being the reasons alleged for Mary, Lady Fane, in her suit for the Barony of Abergavenny in 1587, with other reasons alleged to show that such dignities by custom and reason descend to heirs female, produced on behalf of Anne claiming to be Lady Clifford."

Also, in the same series, April, 1628, there is "The Petition of Anne, Countess-Dowager, late wife of Richard, Earl of Dorset, deceased, and daughter and sole heir of George, Earl of Cumberland, Lord Clifford, Westmoreland and Vescy, to the King. On the death of her father, the titles of Clifford, Westmoreland and Vescy descended to the petitioner, yet Francis, Earl of Cumberland, has published that the name of Lord Clifford and that of Lord Vescy pertain to him; and Henry Clifford, Chivaler, was summoned to this present Parliament, and styles himself Lord Clifford . . . prays the King to admit her claim to the dignities of Clifford, Westmoreland and Vescy, and to order the Earl of Cumberland, and Henry, his son, to forbear to style themselves by these names."

In 1630 she married Philip, Earl of Montgomery, who shortly afterwards became the Earl of Pembroke by the death of his brother, and she again claimed her inheritance, still, however, in vain. In 1641 died her uncle, leaving one son, Henry, and one daughter, Elizabeth, married to the Earl of Cork. Two years later her cousin Henry died without heir male, and without further dispute, Anne stepped into her inheritance, thereby proving her original right. She had not sold it !

" 1644. So by the death of this cousin-german of mine, Henry Clifford, Earl of Cumberland, without heirs male, ye lands of mine inheritance in Craven and Westmoreland reverted unto me without question or controversie after y^t his father Francis, Earl of Cumberland, and this Earl Henry, his son, had unjustly detained from me the antient lands in Craven from ye death of my father and ye lands in Westmoreland from ye death of my mother until this time, yet had I little or no profit from ye estate for some years after by reason of ye civil wars." On the death of her second husband in 1649, she retired to the North, and began to fortify her castles. The Parliamentary forces demolished them, but she said that as often as Cromwell pulled them down she would build them up again. After a time, admiring her spirit, the Protector gave orders she should not be molested. She was not even yet free from litigation, as at first she had troubles with her tenants. In every case, however, through knowledge, experience, and firmness she finally triumphed. A cloth-worker having bought a property held under her by the yearly rent of one hen, he refused to acknowledge her as his Seigneuress by paying that small rent. But she sued him successfully, and though she spent £200, she secured that hen, and the right of which it was the symbol.

She asserted all the privileges connected with her inheritance. In her Diary she says: "As the King came out of Scotland, when he lay at Yorke, there was a striffe between my father and my Lord Burleighe, who was then President, who should carie the sword; but it was adjudged on my father's side, because it was his office by inheritance, and so is lineally descended upon me." She became High Sheriff of Westmoreland also by right of her inheritance, and exercised its duties in person for a time. "The 29th December, 1651, did I sign and seal a patent to Mr. Thomas Gabetis to be my Deputy Sheriff of ye County of Westmoreland."

Looking back on her life in the quiet of her northern home, she said: "I must confess, with inexpressible thankfulness, that I was born a happy creature in mind, body, and fortune, and that those two Lords of mine to whom I was afterwards by the Divine providence married, were in their several kinds worthy noblemen as any were in this Kingdom. Yet was it my misfortune to have contradictions and crosses with them both, with my

first Lord about the desire he had to make me sell my
rights in ye lands of mine inheritance for money, which
I never did nor never would consent unto, insomuch as
this matter was the cause of a long contention betwixt us,
as also for his profuseness in consuming his estate."
Her dispute with her second husband arose because she
would not compel her daughter by her first husband,
against the girl's desire, to marry his son by his first wife.
The consequence of these two disputes, in both of which
she was in the right, was that "the marble halls of Knoll
and the gilded towers of Wilton, were often to me the
Bowers of secret anguish." She was not what has been
called a man's woman, but she was essentially a woman's
woman. All good women were her friends : her cousin,
the Countess of Cork, daughter of her usurping uncle ;
her sister-in-law the Countess of Dorset, wife of her
brother-in-law, whom she considered her greatest enemy.
Though King James was against her, Queen Anne was
her warm friend. She had no children by her second
husband ; and her two sons by Earl Dorset died young.
She had great consolation in the affection, first of her
mother, then of her two daughters, and also of her
grandchildren. It was in connection with one of these
that an important incident occurred, necessary to be fully
explained here.

I have been allowed to utilise some critical points
communicated by me to the *Athenæum*, No. 3475, p.
709, 2nd June, 1894.

In an article on "Letter-writing," published in *The*

World, 5th April, 1753, Sir Horace Walpole quotes the famous and often repeated letter by Anne Clifford, Dowager-Countess of Pembroke, to the Secretary of State, who wanted her to nominate his follower for Appleby :—

"I have been neglected by a Court, I have been bullied by a usurper, but I will not be dictated to by a subject. Your man shan't stand.

"ANNE DORSET, PEMBROKE AND MONTGOMERY."

Lodge and other writers doubt its genuineness. The author of the article in the " Dict. of Nat. Biog." gives as reasons for doubting it that Sir Joseph Williamson, to whom it was supposed to be addressed, was not made Secretary of State until 1674; that Anne died in 1675, and that there was no election between these dates ; also, that it was not in the style of her correspondence, and the signature was unusual, because she always signed her titles in the order of creation—Pembroke, Dorset, and Montgomery—and not in the order of her two marriages. None of the critics, however, seems to have followed out the correspondence in the Domestic Series of " State Papers" at the Public Record Office, which, though it does not include the contested letter, yet illustrates it in a remarkable manner.

The Parliament elected in 1661, 13 Charles II., has been called " The Long or Pensionary Parliament," lasting till 1678. (*See* " Parl. Returns," vol. lxii., Part I., p. 530.) John Lowther, Esq. of Hackthrop, and John Dalston, Esq. of Accornbank, were Burgesses for

Appleby. John Lowther's death necessitated a new election, and in January, 1667-8, there was great excitement in and about Appleby. From Anne's position as High Sheriff of the County, she had the right to nominate a candidate; from her great goodness and bounty to the place, the Corporation were willing to gratify her by electing whom she would. She determined to have one of her grandsons, the Tuftons, sons of her daughter, Countess Thanet, four of whom were over twenty-one, and in need of occupation. Failing them, she meant to have selected her kinsman, Anthony Lowther. But Joseph Williamson, Secretary to Lord Arlington, then Secretary of State, had set his heart on that seat, and by all means in his power, open and underhand, attempted to secure it. He was a native of those parts, and had friends and relatives there, who all bestirred themselves in his favour. Everybody " plied the Countess," Williamson himself, his brother and friends, the neighbouring gentry, the Justices of the Peace, the Bishop of Winchester, Lord Arlington himself. Her replies at first were very kindly, but they gradually became more and more " definite."

Anne's first letter, explaining how her interest was engaged, dated 16th January, 1667-8, was addressed to "Mr. Secretary Williamson at Whitehall," showing that there is no weight in the argument as to Williamson's appointment not taking place till 1674, as being Under-Secretary, he could be addressed so. Further, it is evident that the contested letter was not addressed to Williamson, but to Lord Arlington, about Williamson, though it may certainly have been re-addressed, and sent to him later, and may have been found among his papers.

To Lord Arlington on 17th January, she writes : " Mr Williamson, being of so eminent an ingenuity, cannot miss a Burgess - ship elsewhere." On 25th January, Arlington writes again to her on behalf of his Secretary. On 29th January, George Williamson writes to his brother: " Unless the three Tuftons be taken off by Lady Thanet's means, it is impossible for any man to oppose. . . . Dr. Smith fears the taking off of the old Lady, but if done, we shall be joyful." 4th February, Dan Fleming writes to Williamson about plying the Lady Pembroke: " If you cannot accomplish this, you should stay the Writ as long as you can, until you have a good account of your interest in Appleby." The same day Dr. Smith wrote to Williamson telling him of his friend's work : " The success of it will be seen by her answer to Lord Arlington, whereof she showed me a copy. I cannot see how it is possible to do any good unless her grandchildren be taken off." George Williamson writes same date to his brother, that Lord Arlington had been urging Thomas Tufton to withdraw. " Neither Arlington nor the Bishop make any impression on the wilful Countess." On 6th February, Lord Arlington writes again, to whom Anne replies : " It was myself, and neither my daughter of Thanet, nor any of my children, that made me attempt making one of her sons a Burgess for Appleby." " If it should happen otherwise, I will submit with patience, but never yield my consent. I know very well how powerful a man a Secretary of State is throughout the King's dominions, so am confident that by your Lordship's favour and recommendation you might quickly help this Mr. Williamson to a Burgess-ship without doing wrong or discourtesy to a widow that wants but two years of fourscore, and to her grandchildren, whose father and mother suffered as much in their worldly fortunes for the King as most of his subjects did."

One can see that the spirited old lady has been kindled to white heat, and that very little more would make her say something very like what has been preserved by Walpole.

As to her style, she employed a Secretary, Mr. Sedgwick. That Secretary was absent from Skipton Castle for a few days at this time. It is just possible that the young candidate, Thomas Tufton, himself became her clerk on the occasion, and transmitted his grandmother's words as he thought she said them, without anything of Sedgwick's clerkly polish.

On 9th February, George Williamson writes to his brother, enclosing a letter from Dr. Smith : " If the town be left to their own freedom, your brother will carry it, but I doubt that the Countess will never let it come to that, being resolved to present one to them. If none of her grandchildren will accept, she will pitch upon Anthony Lowther. She has been heard to say that if they all refuse, she will stand for it herself, by which you may imagine what the issue is likely to be."

K

13th February, Sir John Lowther to Williamson says that he had taken off his kinsman from the candidature. "I believe that her Ladyship will prevail in her resolution with regard to her relatives," "and will neither desire, seek, nor need, anybody's help to make whom she desires. I know this by a letter from the Mayor."

23rd February, Thomas Gabetis, Under-Sheriff, writes to Mr. Williamson that he studied to serve him, but the Countess had planned otherwise. "The Corporation being disposed to gratify her for her great nobleness and bounty to the place. My station obligates me to render service with obedience to her commands, especially in this particular."

Here comes the period at which the undated letter preserved by Walpole might well have been written. But between him and the printers it seems to have disappeared. There is no further letter now on the subject among the State Papers.

But in her Diary, Harl. MS. 6177, f. 180, she writes: "And on ye second day of March in this year my grandchild, Mr. Thomas Tufton, was chosen Burgess of ye Town of Appleby to serve in the House of Commons in Parliament therein assembled, and sitting in Parliament at Westminster, in ye place of Mr. John Lowther, my cosin's son, who dyed; so as Mr. Thomas Tufton, my grandchild, begann first of all to sitt in ye said House of Commons at Westminster as a member thereof, the 10th day of March, he being ye first grandchild of mine yt ever sate in ye House of Commons" (1668).

On 21st September, 1668, in 1670, and in 1674, this Mr. Thomas Tufton visited his grandmother and his constituency, still Burgess.

So she had her way with the Secretary of State, as she had had with the King, the Protector, and her noble husbands. Her motto, it may be remembered, was, "Preserve your loyalty, defend your rights."

Many other women have been right in their contentions, but to very few have been given, with the spirit and courage, the wealth, power, patience and opportunity to secure success. Her struggle was no purely personal one; it was the first Protest against the invasion of the rights of her sex. She saw how "legal precedent" was drifting.

Mr. Joshua Williams, on Land Settlement, shows something of the history of the changes. (*See* "Judicial Papers," vol i., Part I., and Sir Harris Nicolas, "Extinct Peerages.")

I have already noted the decision of Judge Popham in the case of Lady Fane, which Anne Clifford quoted as precedent for her own case in vain.

She utilised every opportunity of improving herself and blessing her fellow creatures, and she would not go where she could do no good. Being invited to the Court of Charles II., she replied : "I could not go, unless I were to wear blinkers like my horses !"

Dr. Donne said of her, that she "was able to converse on any subject, from predestination to slea-silk."

In her Funeral Sermon, preached by Bishop Rainbow,

he mentioned her learning, hospitality, and encouragement of letters, and reckoned among her many virtues, Courage, Humility, Faith, Charity, Piety, Wisdom. "Thus died this great wise Woman, who, while she lived, was the Honour of her Sex and her Age, fitter for a History than a Sermon." 1676.

In 1694 Mary Astell protested against the state of things in her day in a small anonymous publication, "A Serious Proposal to the Ladies, by a Lover of their Sex." Speaking of the repute learning was held in about 150 years before, she says: "It was so very modish that the fair Sex seemed to believe that Greek and Latin added to their charms, and Plato and Aristotle untranslated were frequent ornaments of their closets. One would think by the effects that it was a proper way of educating them, since there are no accounts in history of so many great women in any one age as are between 1500 and 1600." She refers to Mr. Wotton's "Reflections on Ancient and Modern Learning," p. 349, and makes clear that her proposal is to found an institution for the higher education of women, to be dedicated to the Princess Anne of Denmark. In 1696 she also published "An Essay in Defence of the Female Sex, by a Lady." Defoe next year, in his "Essays on Projects," proposed to establish Academies for women, and criticises "the Lady" who had suggested the idea under the conditions of a Monastery. Nevertheless, a second edition of her first book appeared in 1695, and a third in 1697.

" Reflections upon Marriage " appeared in 1700. In the third edition of the latter, 1706, answering objections, in the Preface, she says : " These reflections have no other design than to correct some abuses which are none the less because power and prescription seem to authorise them. 'Tis a great fault to submit to Authority when we should only yield to Reason," . . . " designing nothing but the Public Good, and to return, if possible, the native Liberty, the Rights and Privileges of the Subject. . . . She did not indeed advise women to think man's folly wisdom, nor his brutality that love and worship he promised in the matrimonial oath, for this required a flight of wit and sense much above her poor ability, and proper only to masculine understandings. . . . 'Tis true, through want of learning and of that superior genius which men, as men, lay claim to, she was ignorant of the natural inferiority of our sex, which our masters lay down as a self-evident and fundamental truth. She saw nothing in the reason of things to make this either a principle or a conclusion, but very much to the contrary, it being Sedition, at least, if not Treason, to assert it in this Reign (*i.e.*, the reign of Queen Anne). For if by *the natural superiority of their Sex* they mean that every man is superior to every woman, which is the obvious meaning, and that which must be stuck to if they would speak sense, it would be a sin in any woman to have dominion over any man, and the greatest Queen ought not to command, but to obey her Footman, because no municipal Laws can supersede or change the Laws of Nature. If they mean that some men are superior to some women, that is no great discovery. Had they turned the tables they would have found that some women are superior to some men. Or, had they remembered their Oath of Allegiance and Supremacy, they might have known that one woman is superior to all the men in the Kingdom, or else they have sworn to very little purpose, and it must not be supposed that their Reason and Religion would suffer them to take oaths contrary to the Law of Nature and the Reason of things." "That the Custom of the World has put women, generally speaking, into a state of subjection, is not denied; but the right can be no more proved by the fact than the predominance of vice can justify it. They say that Scripture shows that women were in a state of subjection. So were the Jews, under the Chaldeans; and the Christians under the Romans. Were they necessarily inferior? That ingenious theorist, Mr. Whiston, argues, 'that before the Fall woman was the superior.' Woman is put into the world to serve God. The service she owes a man at any time is only a business by-the-bye, just as it may be any man's business to keep hogs. He was not made for this, but if he hires himself out to such an employment, he ought conscientiously to perform it. . . . We do not find any man think any the worse of his understanding because another has more physical power, or conclude himself less capable for any post because he has not been preferred to it. . . . If all men are born Free, how are all women born slaves? Not Milton himself would cry up Liberty for Female Slaves, or plead the Lawfulness of resisting a private Tyranny. . . . If mere power gives a right to rule, there can be no such thing as Usurpation, but a High-wayman, so long as he has Strength to force, has also a right to command our obedience. Strength of mind goes along with Strength of body, and 'tis only for some odd accidents, which philosophers have not yet thought worth while to inquire into, that the sturdiest porter is not also the wisest man. . . . Sense is a portion that God has been pleased to distribute to both sexes with an impartial hand; but learning is what men have engrossed to themselves, and one cannot but admire their improvements." She winds up with another Eulogy on the good Queen Anne. But society did not then reform itself upon her suggestions.

Before the close of the eighteenth century (1792), however, **Mary Wollstonecraft blew a loud trumpet blast,** in her indignant "Vindication of the Rights of Women." She treats the subject on lines that men and women are only now beginning to learn to read. (*See* Dedication, p. x.) "There can be no duty without reason. There can be no morality without equality. There can be no justice when its recipients are only of one sex." "Let us first consider women in the grand light of human creatures, who, in common with men, are placed on this earth to unfold their faculties." "Who made man the exclusive judge, if woman partakes with him the gift of reason?" "Do you not act a tyrant's part when you *force* all women, by denying them civil and political rights, to remain immured in their families, groping in the dark? Surely you will not assert that a duty can be binding which is not founded on reason." "Women may be convenient slaves, but slavery will have its constant effect, degrading the master and the abject dependent." "It is time to effect a revolution in female manners, time to restore to women their lost dignity and to make them labour, by reforming themselves, to reform the world." She was too much in advance of her times to be successful in spreading her views, especially as they were entangled with other opinions even more unpopular in her day. Yet she sowed the seed that is still growing. The society she pictures gives a painful illustration of the effects of the exclusively masculine creeds of her century.

Yet, during that dark age of women's privilege, there were some **Legal Cases tried** and decided, refreshing in their results, as they showed that dispassionate judges could still do something for women, when they followed the ordinary principles of Philology, and decreed that a common term could stand for woman as well as for man, even when it meant a privilege.

" A woman was appointed by the Justices to be a *governor of a workhouse* at Chelmsford in Essex, and Mr. Parker moved to quash the order because it was an office not suitable to her sex," but the Court upheld the appointment (2 Lord Raymond's Reports, 1014). "Lady Broughton was *keeper of the Gatehouse Prison*" at Westminster (3 Keble, 32).* "The office of Clerk of the Crown in the King's Bench was granted to a woman" (*see* Showers's Reports of Parliament Cases. Olive *v.* Ingram, 7 Modern Reports, 270).

* In reference to the keepers of prisons, we may note from Rev. J. C. Cox's " Three Centuries of Derbyshire Annals."

" In the Borough of Derby, from an entry made at the Epiphany Sessions, 1732, we see that the County Prisoners were then in the custody. of a female gaoler. . . . 'It was ordered that Mrs. Mary Greatorex, widow, keeper of the gaol for this County, do give account upon oath at next general sessions, what means she has used towards the retaking Elias Wheldon and George Hamblet and John Bradshaw, committed to her custody '" (vol. i., p. 10).

"Among the keepers of the lesser prisons also, we find women. On the death of Thomas Sharman, Keeper of the House of Correction, he was succeeded by his daughter. On the daughter's death Thomas Walker received the appointment, and when Walker died in 1695, the Justices were asked to appoint his married daughter, Mrs. Taylor, the precedent of Sharman's daughter being urged. Sir Robert Wilmot wrote to his brother Justices 11th July, 1695. ' I am earnestly sollicited by this bearer, Mrs. Taylor, daughter of Mr. Walker, late Master of ye House of Correction, to recommend her to your favour to have the Office to be continued to her for some few years until her son is of age to perform and execute the same as she hath done for this 7 or 8 years last past, during which time her father, Mr. Walker, hath been very infirm and helpless, and farther also affirmed that it is very well knowne yt she is more than ordinarily qualified to oversee and direct those under her charge in such employments and manifactures as is most proper to employ them in. My humble opinion would have been, if I had been so well as to have waited upon you at Bakewell, yt she would probably, by reason of her long experience, execute ye office as well, or better than any a stranger thereto, and it would be of some conveniency that she is in possession of a house fitted for ye purpose, for this County, as I take it hath no County House as others have provided at ye charge of ye County. But my opinion, together with my humble service here presented, is wholly submitted to your judgment.' " The result of this has not been recorded, p. 30.

A lady's appointment to be *Commissioner of Sewers* was also discussed by Callis, who " decided that as the office by statute " shall be granted to such *person* or persons as the said Lords should appoint, " the word *person* stands indifferently for either sex . . . and though women have been discreetly spared, . . . yet I am of opinion, for the authorities and reasons aforesaid, that this appointment is *warrantable by the law.* Women have been secluded as unfit, yet they are not in law to be excluded as incapable," *i.e.,* the election determined eligibility. So the Countess of Warwick was allowed to retain the benefits of her election. (*See* R. Callis on Sewers, 253.)

In Hilary Term, 1739, the case of Olive *v.* Ingram (7 Mod. Reports, 263-274), was heard before Sir William Lee, Chief-Justice; Sir Francis Page, Sir Edmund Probyn, Sir William Chapple, and Justices, to decide whether a woman could vote for a sexton, and whether she could be a sexton. A woman candidate for the office of sexton of the Church of St. Botolph without Bishopsgate had 169 *indisputable* votes and 40 *women's votes;* the plaintiff had 174 indisputable votes and 22 women's votes. The woman had been declared elected. (2 Strange, 1114.)

The case was considered so important that it was heard five times. First, whether a woman could vote? The counsel against argued that women could not vote in this case, as they did not do so in others ; that they did not vote for members of Parliament, quoting Coke (4 Institute, 4, 5.) The counsel for argued that non-user did not imply inability ; that women paying Scot and Lot had a right to vote on municipal affairs ; that they voted in the great Companies ; that it had been decided in Attorney-General *v.* Nicholson, Trinity Term, 1 George II., that women had a right to elect a preacher. If they could elect to a higher office, how could they not do so to a lower ? It had been decided in Holt *v.* Lyle and Catharine *v.* Surry, according to Hakewell, " that a *feme sole*, if she has a freehold, may vote for a Parliament man." Women did come to the old County Courts, though not compellable thereto. It was a just rule that those who contributed to maintain the elected should themselves be electors. There is a difference between exemption and incapacity. Justice Chapple said, " Women are *sui juris* till they are married."

The Lord Chief-Justice mentioned the case of Holt *v.* Lyle, but added that as he was not bound now to say whether a woman could vote for a Parliament man, he would reserve that point for further consideration. The question here is, whether a woman can be included in "all *persons* paying Scot and Lot." If women are qualified to pay Scot and Lot, they are qualified to keep a sexton. They who pay must determine to whom they will pay. He decided that women could vote for a sexton. Justice Page agreed with Chief-Justice Lee on the general question, but added : " I see no disability in a woman from voting for a Parliament man." Justice Probyn agreed that they who pay have a right to nominate. It *might be thought* that it required an *improved understanding* for a woman to vote for a

Parliament man, but the case of Holt *v.* Lyle was a very strong case.

The woman having thus secured a majority of "indisputable votes," the next question was, Could she hold office ? The objection was that women could not hold places of trust, of exertion, of anything to do with a church.

Chief-Justice Lee said a woman is allowed to be a Constable, and a Keeper of a Prison. Serjeant Wynne said, very high offices have been held by Ladies. The office of Champion at the last Coronation was in a woman. The office of Clerk of the Crown in the King's Bench was granted to a woman. In regard to the Church, women have been allowed to baptise ; there have been Deaconesses, and female servants *circa sacra.* (Romans xvi. 21.) Women have presented to churches. C. J. Lee decided that a woman *could be sexton.* The others concurred. ("Modern Reports," vol. vii., p. 263.)

Strange, the opposing counsel, in reporting the case shortly and confusingly, says that he knew many women sextons at the time. (*See* Strange's Reports, vol. ii., p. 1114.)

In the case of Regina *v.* Chardstock (16 Viner's Abridgment, 414), where "the parish was obstinate in not having another Overseer than a woman," Justice Powell had testily declared that a woman cannot be Oversee of the Poor, that there *can be no custom of the parish to appoint her, because it is an Office* * *created by Act*

* Yet before the said creation of the Statute (43 Eliz.), even in 7 Eliz. there were Overseers of the poor in Westminster (*see* my article, *Athenæum*, No. 3458, p. 148, 3rd February, 1894).

of Parliament. To the petitioner's election he replied that there was *not to be a woman Overseer.* (This case is referred to as "The Queen *v.* Henley" in 7 Modern Reports), and it was reversed in the King's Bench in 1788 in Rex *v.* Stubbs. "Can a woman be Overseer of the Poor?" The only qualification necessary by the Statute (43 Eliza.) is that the Overseer be "a substantial householder." A woman can be "a substantial householder, and therefore she is eligible." Justice Ashhurst referred to the other offices that women had held, as quoted above. "This office has no reference to sex. The only question is whether there be anything in the nature of the office that should make a woman incompetent, and we think *there is not*" (2 Durnford and East's "Term Reports," p. 395).*

* A curious point of appeal with regard to the appointment of Overseer comes to light when women had been chosen for office. The first instance of a female Churchwarden was in 1684 (under the Statute of 1594 all Churchwardens were Overseers of the Poor). (The Rev. J. C. Cox in his "Three Centuries of Derbyshire Annals," vol. i.)

"Upon hearyng Mr. Turner, Attorney, on behalf of Mary Jaques of Draycolt, who informed this Court that the Minister and inhabitants of the Parish of Little Wilne had elected the said Mary Jaques to be one of the Churchwardens of the said Parish, and being alledged by the said Mr. Turner, that she, as a woman was not capable of that office, nor by law compellable to serve it, and therefore prayed the order of the Court to dischardge her from the same. It is thereupon ordered that the said Mary Jaques be freed and dischardged from the said office, and that the Minister and inhabitants of said Parish do forthwith proceed to a newe election." In 1695, the Court on appeal distinctly affirmed the incapacity of a woman to serve. "Ordered by this Court that Mrs. Elizabeth Sleigh and William Mellone bee discharged from serving

Yet before the time that male rivals contested the election with a woman, women had exercised the office without objection. "In the township of Gorton, parish of Manchester, 1748, Widow Waterhouse was overseer of the poor. In 1775 Sarah Schofield played the flute in the chapel choir. In 1826 Mary Grimston was appointed sexton. In 1829 the vestry sent for Ruth Walker to come and break stones" ("Notes and Queries," 5th series, vol. vi., p. 269). In the Parish Register, Totterridge, Middlesex, 2nd March, 1802, entry—burial. Mrs. Elizabeth King, widow, for 46 years Clerk of this Parish, in her 91st year. *Note.*—As long as she was able she attended, and with great strength and pleasure to her hearers, read prayers (p. 493). Mrs. Anne Bass of Ayleston, Leicestershire, an excellent churchwarden for many years. "Notes and Queries," 5th series, vol. iv., 269, 493.*)

the Office of Overseer of the Poor of Hartington Parish, shee being a woman, incapacitated to serve that Office, and William Mellone having served the Office the year last past." Other two men were appointed. (Toulmin Smith, however, says in his "Parish," p 151, "A woman can be appointed as Overseer, and will be compellable to serve.") Precedent, however, did not rule in Derby. We find at Easter Sessions, 1712, on the motion of Mr. Balguy, "Whereas Mrs. Elizabeth Eyre, widow, late Officer of Woodland in this County, is considerably out of Pockett, since she served ye Offices of Headborow and Overseer of the Poor of the said Liberty, and that several persons neglect and refuse to pay the assessment, this Court doth therefore order, and it is hereby ordered that the accounts of the said Mrs. Elizabeth Eyre be laid before ye Justices of this County at their next monthly meeting for the Hundred of High Peake, or before any two Justices of the same Hundred at any other time before or after the said monthly meeting."

* Dr. Cox also tells us in vol. i., p. 112, that there are "Three

The opening of the nineteenth century was signalised by the cessation of the Napoleonic wars ; and the Peace brought wider opportunities of leisure, learning, and literature to both sexes. Yet so powerful had become the force of Custom in confusing men's ideas of Justice, that even James Mill, the pupil of Jeremy Bentham, in his masterly article on " Government " for the Supplement to the " Cyclopædia Britannica " (afterwards republished

references in the Constabulary papers to a woman being nominated. In 1649, Humphrey Hurd, Constable of Osmaston by Ashburne, presents Elizabeth Hurd, Widow, for the Office in the ensuing year, ' she having a sufficient man to her son to serve the office.' But the son refused to serve, and Humphrey Hurd prays the Court to grant an order to bring Elizabeth herself to the next session of the Justices of the Peace to take the oath."

" On 3rd April, 1649, John Burton, Constable of Linton, presents Elizabeth Taylor, Widdow, for to be constable for this year next ensuing, and hee with the rest of the inhabitants of Linton aforesaid (18 in number), whose names are hereunder written, sheweth that our town custom hath ever been a gone-by house, and that now it falleth upon that house, according to our ancient custom, wherefore our humble request to the Honourable Bench is that they would bee pleased to take it into consideration and give order that shee may officiate, and execute the said office according to the ancient custom." In 1683, however, when the inhabitants of Sinfin and Arleston presented to the Court, Clare Clay, Widow, " to take upon her the Office of a Constable," the Justices ordered her to be discharged, and continued the last constable in Office " till he present another more fit person to succeed him."

Of course it is possible this special widow may have been infirm or unsuitable for other reasons than sex. In Olive *v.* Ingram (7 Modern Reports), pp. 263-274, it had been found that women were eligible for and even compellable to serve the Office ; and it was added, " A Constable was once a Great Peace Officer, how contemptible soever he may be thought at present." (*See* also T. C. Anstey's " Supposed Constitutional Restraints," p. 24.)

in pamphlet form, 1825) could allow it to blind his eyes
to the logical results of his own reasoning. In page 494
he says : " That one human being will desire to render
the person and property of another subservient to his
pleasures, notwithstanding the pain or loss of pleasure
which it may occasion to that other individual, *is the
foundation of government.* The desire of the object im-
plies the desire of the power necessary to accomplish the
object. The desire, therefore, of that power which is
necessary to render the persons and properties of other
human beings subservient to our pleasures, is a grand
governing law of human nature." Yet the writer of this
searching analysis of the cause and need of government
says elsewhere (p. 300) : " One thing is pretty clear, that
all those individuals whose interests are indisputably
included in those of other individuals, may be struck off
from political rights without inconvenience. In this light
may be viewed all children up to a certain age, whose
interests are involved in those of their parents. In this
light, also, women may be regarded, the interests of
almost all of whom is involved in either that of their
fathers or that of their husbands." Yet even at that
early date a man, inspired by a woman, rose up to protest against this sweeping assertion. William Thompson,
in 1825, published a little book dedicated to Mrs.
Wheeler, that puts the whole question in a broad modern
light, " *The Appeal* of one Half of the Human Race,
Women, against the Pretentions of the other Half, Men,
to retain them in Political, and thence in Civil and

Domestic Slavery. In reply to a paragraph of Mr. Mill's celebrated article on Government." This interesting book was the first voice of a nineteenth century man against the degradation of women. He points out that Mill has not nearly reached the level of his master, Bentham, in his conception. He asks, what is to become of those not included in the "nearly all"? what of those that are? "Why are women's interests included in those of men? Mr. Mill's article seeks to evade the equal claims of the other half of the human race to similar protection against the abuse of the same power, against the application of the general principle of security to women." "In order to include women in the proscription of children, a fiction must be manufactured, as none of the good reasons applicable to children would be found to apply to women, and this romance of an identity of interest is the ingenious, say rather, the vulgar, the audacious fiction devised" (p. 15). "From this examination it results that the pretext set up to exclude women from political rights, namely, the inclination of men to use power over them beneficently; would, if admitted, sweep away the grand argument itself for the political rights of men." "We shall investigate the philosophical pretext of the 'article' for the degradation of one half of the adult portion of the human race in the following order :—(1) Does the identity of interest between men and women, in point of fact, exist? (2) If it does exist, is it a sufficient cause, or any reason at all, why either of the parties, with interests thus

L

identified, should therefore be deprived of political rights? (3) Is there in the nature of things any security for equality of enjoyments proportional to exertion and capabilities, but by means of equal civil rights? or any security for equal civil, but by means of equal political rights? In regard to the first, there are three great classes of women. First, all women without fathers or husbands; second, adult daughters in their father's establishment; third, wives. The first class have no men to identify their interests with; they are therefore the class, sometimes scornfully, called *the unprotected.* Adult daughters can acquire legal rights as against their fathers, but on marriage they forfeit their freedom, and are again thrown back into the class of children or idiots." " Involving of interests must mean that one enjoys as much as the other, is this true as between husband and wife?" "The very assumption of despotic power by the husbands over wives is in itself a demonstration, that in the opinion of husbands, a contrariety, and not an involving of interests, exists between them and their wives. Domestic despotism corrupts man's moral frame." "If it is more difficult for women to labour, why should men further increase the difficulty by protecting themselves? In justice to the stronger excluding party, as well as to the weaker, all such powers of excluding ought to be withheld" (p. 149).

Many must have read, but few assimilated Mr. Thompson's able and generous arguments.

Meanwhile, in regard to the Representation of the

People's Acts, the Parliamentary franchises had been revised and cobbled, but in none was any but the general term used. The Act 7 and 8 William III., c. 7., describes electors as "freeholders," or "persons"; 18 George II., c. 18., 19 George II., c. 28., use the same general terms. That of 3 George III., c. 15., not to extend to London and Norwich, limits the franchise "to persons who had taken up their freedom for 12 months."

Those of 11 George III., c. 55 for New Shoreham; 22 George III., c. 31 for Cricklade; 44 George III., c. 60 for Aylesbury; 11 George IV. and 1 William IV., c. 74 for East Retford, confer the suffrage on "*every* Freeholder being above the age of 21 years, or on inhabitant householders of same age." There is no term ever used that might not include a woman. But just at the time when the tide of civilisation and education was beginning to rise again, just after "The Appeal of Women" had appeared, by W. Thompson and Mrs. Wheeler (1825), all historical precedent was reversed. Concentrated social *opinion* became boldly expressed in *law*.

In the Reform Bill of 1832, the word "male" was interpolated before "persons" in the Charters of the newly created Boroughs. Never before, and never since has the phrase "male persons" appeared in any Statute of the Realm. By this Act, therefore, women were technically disfranchised for the first time in the history of the English Constitution. The privilege of abstention was converted into the penalty of exclusion. Curiously enough, the framers seemed to have had dim notions of this, as in all reference to older Charters the term "person" only appeared, and the interpolating adjective "male" is suppressed. Therefore in Boroughs holding by older Charters women were not necessarily excluded, except by the reflex action of the 1832 Statute. (*See* 2 and 3 William IV., c. xlv., ss. 24, 25, 31, 32, and 33.)

In strange contrast to the spirit of this Act were the Bills passed in 1833 and 1834, which gave freedom, at the nation's expense, to all Colonial slaves.

The first result of the extinction of women's liberty was the passing of the Bill which took away their immemorial right of *Dower* (2 and 3 Will. IV., c. 105), which practically gives to husbands the right to leave their wives and children penniless.

The Municipal Franchises naturally followed the example of the Parliamentary one, and in spite of Charter, and in spite of precedent, limited their privileges to "male persons." (Municipal Corporations Act, 1835.)

For many years these readings remained in uncontested force, not without protest on the part of women and of the friends of justice. In 1850 Lord Brougham's Act (13 and 14 Victoria, c. 21), "for shortening the language used in Acts of Parliament," was passed. This enacted that "words importing the masculine gender shall be deemed to include females," except where otherwise expressly stated. Next year the Earl of Carlisle presented a Petition drafted at a public meeting in Sheffield for the extension of the Parliamentary Suffrage to women. Sympathetic minds were stirred by the great American Convention on the subject, and in the *Westminster and Foreign Quarterly*, July, 1851, appears the notable article on "The Enfranchisement of Women," by Mrs. Mill. "That women have as good a claim as men have to the suffrage and to be jury, it would be difficult for anyone to deny." "It is one axiom of English freedom that taxation and representation always go together; it is another that all persons must be tried by their peers, yet *both* are denied to women." "A reason must be given why what is permitted to one person is interdicted to another." "Far from being *expedient*, the division of mankind into two castes, one born to rule the other, is an unqualified mischief, a source of perversion and demoralisation both to the favoured class and to those at whose expense they are favoured, producing none of the good which it is the custom to ascribe to it, and forming a bar to any really vital improvement either in the character or the social condition of the human race."

"It is the boast of modern Europeans and Americans that they know and do many things which their fore-fathers neither knew nor did; it is the most unquestion-able point of their superiority that custom is not now the tyrant that it formerly was. Yet in this case prejudice appeals to custom and authority." "Great thinkers, from Plato to Condorcet, have made emphatic protests in favour of the equality of women." "We deny the right of any portion of the species to decide for another portion, or any individual for another individual, what is and what is not their 'proper sphere.' The proper sphere of all human beings is the largest and highest they can attain to."

"Women could vote in the East India Company, the South Sea Company, and the Bank of England. In the first, it was voting for directors with power of life and death, taxation, imprisonment and banishment, over hundreds of thousands of English - born men, and a hundred millions of Indian-born men" (Sydney Smith's "Enfranchisement of Woman the Law of the Land").

The Bill of 1867.—Again the "Representation of the people" came before the House in 1867 (30 and 31 Vict., c. 102). The word "man" was exchanged for "male persons" of the 1832 Charter. John Stuart Mill redeemed his father's errors and moved an Amendment that it should be made expressly to include women. "We ought not to deny to them what we are conceding to everyone else, a right to be consulted; of having, what every petty trade or profession has, a few members who feel specially called on to attend to their interests, to point out how these interests are affected by law." "The want of this protection has affected their interests vitally. The rich can make private laws unto themselves by settlements, but what of the poor?"

"Educational endowments founded for both sexes have been limited to boys. The medical profession shuts its doors when women strive to enter in. The Royal Academy shut its doors when women began to distinguish themselves. There is no meaning in the objection that women have no time to attend to politics. Do all enfranchised men take time?" "What is the meaning of political freedom? Is it anything but the control of those that make politics by those who do not?" (p. 7). His Amendment was lost. But so also was the Amendment that the phrase "male persons" of 1832 should be replaced. The Bill enacted that every man of full age, and not subject to legal incapacity, "duly qualified and registered," should have the right to vote. During the discussion, the Hon. G. Denman, Justice of the Common Pleas, asked the following question—"Why, instead of the words 'male person' of the Act of 1832, the word 'man' had been substituted in the present Bill? In the fifth clause of the Bill he found that after saying that every 'man' should be entitled to be registered, it proceeds to say, '*or a male person* in any university who has passed any senior middle examination.' In the light of Lord Brougham's Act, if the Court of Queen's Bench had to decide to-morrow on the construction of these clauses they *would be constrained* to hold that they *conferred the* suffrage on *female persons* as well as on males." The Government did not answer the question, but it passed the Bill as it stood. T. Chisholm Anstey on "The New Reform Act, 1867," p. 87, says: "No Law, Custom, prescription, determination is against the right of women . . . In not one of the Boroughs where Suffrage was regulated by 'Charter' or 'Custom' or prescription, or even where it was regulated by a local Act of Parliament, can there be found one instance of any provision or usage whatsoever, whereby any voter was excluded from the enjoyment of the suffrage by reason of sex" (p. 90). Whitelock says: "By the Custom of England, women are not returned of juries, nor put into Offices or Commission, nor are they eligible to serve in Parliament, or admitted to be members of the House of Peers, but, by reason of their sex, they are *exempted* from such employments." The omission of the Electoral Franchise from that enumeration is remarkable. If women were at that time considered to be excluded, by any custom of England, from the Parliamentary Franchise, as well as from Parliament, it is scarcely conceivable that Whitelock should have omitted to mention so important a fact. There is no trace of such in record or report, except in the one phrase of Coke. This Act, therefore, to ordinary as well as to logical minds, seemed to reinstate women in their ancient though neglected privileges, which the advance of education had taught them now to appreciate. Therefore, next year, 5,374 women had themselves duly registered in the town of Manchester alone, in the neighbouring town of Salford about 1,500, and large numbers in other places. Great uncertainty prevailed as to how to treat them, but most of the revising barristers threw them out. Where they were left on the Register, some of them really did vote, as "Warren on Election Law," p. 175, had made clear that when a woman's name got by mistake on the

Register, her vote must be accepted. Even in Manchester, whose Charter and whose case decided against women, Mrs. Lily Maxwell voted. The Manchester women consolidated their claims and appealed against the decision.

The Times, 3rd November, 1868: "The present position of the Women's Suffrage question is decidedly an odd one. It is not often that the glorious uncertainty of the law is so strikingly illustrated as it has been by the decision of the revising barristers, as to whether a woman, under certain assumed conditions, may, or may not, vote for a Member of Parliament. . . . According to one view—the view of the majority—she may vote if her name is on the electoral register and is not objected to, the revising barrister himself remaining neutral; according to another, the barrister ought himself, if necessary, to start the objection. According to a third —the view taken in four courts—her name ought to remain on the electoral roll even although objected to. However, this uncertainty is very soon to cease . . . if one supposes it was ever the intention of the Legislature to give women a vote, and if they do get it, it will be by a sort of accident, in itself objectionable, though in its practical consequences perhaps harmless enough. On the other hand, if they are refused it, the nation will, no doubt, be formally and in the light of day committing itself, through its judicial tribunal to the dangerous doctrine that representation need not go along with taxation."

The case of **Chorlton** *v.* **Lings**, L. R. 4 C. P., p. 374,
was heard before the Court of Common Pleas in Westminster, 7th and 9th November, 1868, Lord Chief-
Justice Bovill and Justices Willes, Byles and Keating
sitting on the Bench. The facts can be found in the
Law Reports, and it is good that they should be recalled
to the minds of the rising generation, as they show how
Sex-Bias can blind the eyes of Justice.

They are treated in a more lively manner in the pages
of *The Times*, 9th and 10th November. Mr. Coleridge,
Q.C., and Dr. Pankhurst appeared on behalf of the
women, Mr. Mellish, Q.C., against. Miss Becker, the
woman's champion, was present, and many other ladies.
Mr. Coleridge stated that there were 5,347 women duly
registered in the town of Manchester, qualified *except by
sex* to be electors. The Chief-Justice asked him if he
had found any cases of women exercising political
privileges before then? He said he had not!* But he
added that the Statute for the County Courts *might* have
included both sexes. The Chief-Justice interpolated,
"The Common Law existed before the Statute Law.
There is no trace, so far as I know, of women having
been admitted to the assemblies of the wise men of the
land!"† (Laughter.) Mr. Coleridge gave the examples
of the Countess of Westmoreland voting by attorney
and Mrs. Copley signing the indenture. Justice Willes
interposed, "She might have been a returning officer,
which office she unquestionably might fill!"‡ Mr.

* *See* Ante. to the contrary, p. 64. † p. 10. ‡ p. 70.

Coleridge then quoted Luders as to the women burgesses of Lyme Regis; the Statute of Henry VI., which limited suitors to forty shilling freeholders and the citizen burgesses, as all being enacted of "chusers" or "electors" in common terms. Hallam (Con. Hist., ch. xiii.), states that "all Householders paying Scot and Lot, and Local Rates, voted for members of Parliament." Women could be freeholders, householders, citizens, burgesses, suitors, taxpayers, therefore they could vote. It is true that the Reform Bill of 1832 read these as only applied to "male persons," but the Bill of 1867 used the term "man," while Lord Brougham's Act had decided the term "man" should include woman, unless where it was otherwise expressly stated. It was not "otherwise expressly stated" in the Statute of 1867. There was no legal restraint against women voting, and he quoted the case of Holt *v.* Lyle, which affirmed that a *feme sole* had a right to vote for a Parliament man.

Mr. Mellish, in opposition, said that Manchester was a new Borough in 1832, and claimed by its Charter the franchise for "male persons." The Bill of 1867 stated that it would not alter existing franchises. The ground of women being excluded was their *legal incapacity*. It is true no statute took their right away, because they never had had it! "As well suitors as others," of Statute 52 Henry III., c. 10, did not necessarily mean women. "They could not be Esquires or Knights." Justice Willes interposing—"Not only in Books of Romance but in Books of Chivalry we see they can!" "The case quoted by Mr. Coleridge is valueless. If a lady were not present to vote, it was clearly illegal for her to do so by attorney. Mrs. Copley was Patron of the Borough, and probably acted as returning officer. In Olive *v.* Ingram the majority of the Judges were against the woman's claim.* Peeresses could not sit in the House of Lords." Justice Willes interposing—"Yet peeresses marrying commoners, the commoners became Peers, and sat *jure mariti.* Is not that, at least, representative of a woman?"† Mr. Mellish then referred to the parallel case that had been tried in Scotland, Brown *v.* Ingram

---

* The assertion does not seem borne out by the case *in extenso,* though it does by the short and misleading report in 2 Strange, 1114, the counsel for the opposition. As Strange also affirmed that women could not hold by military tenure, his judgment regarding them on other points may well be doubted.

† It is clear that *women often conferred the Parliamentary franchise on their husbands.* Thus Justice Powys in Ashby *v.* White, 2 Lord Raymond's Reports, 943, said, "I know *Ludlow* a borough, where all the burgesses' daughters' husbands have a right to vote." By statute, 20 George III., c. 17 (A.D. 1780), "An Act to remove certain Difficulties relative to Voters at County Elections," it was enacted by section 12, "that where any Woman, the Widow of any Person, Tenant in Fee or in Tail, shall be entitled to Dower or Thirds, by the Common Law, out of the Freehold Estate of which her Husband died seised or possessed of, and shall intermarry with a second Husband, such second Husband shall be entitled to vote in respect of such Dower or Thirds, if such Dower or Thirds shall be of the clear yearly Value of forty Shillings, or upwards, although the same has not been assigned or set out by Metes or Bounds, if such second Husband shall be in the actual receipt of the profits of such Dower, and the Estate from whence the same issues is rated to, and contributes to the Land-tax in the name of the actual owners of the Lands and Tenements from whence such Dower or Thirds arises or issues."

(7 Court of Session Cases, 3rd Series, 281.) Judgment was against the women, first, because they were legally incapacitated; and second, because to *give* them a vote would be against public policy, as it was a premium on ladies to remain unmarried in order to retain their votes, and a premium to them to desire that their husbands might die in order that they might become enfranchised as widows. Mr. Coleridge said that the Scotch case had no bearing on this. Lord Chief-Justice Bovill was obliged to concede that "it is quite true that a few women being parties to indentures of returns of members of Parliament have been shown, and it is quite possible that there may have been some other instances in early times of women having voted and assisted in legislation. Indeed, such instances are mentioned by Selden. Yet the fact of the right not having been asserted for centuries raises a very strong presumption against its ever having had legal existence."* And though he acknowledged that in many statutes "man" may be properly held to include women, he decided against this interpretation here. The rest of the judges agreed with him. "A woman had no *locus standi.*"

One of the arguments against women was, that even if the word "Man" could be proved to include "Woman," they must consider not the words, but the *intention* of the framers, an argument that could never

* The last recorded example of women proffering their vote was in 1640, less than 260 years before (p. 107). While Amersham and other towns had not voted for 321 years (p. 98).

further argued that the word "men" could not be said constitutionally to include "women," and that they must bring forward a statute proving their right as such. Since the 2nd edition of this book, I have found such a statute, which proves the judges and the opposing Counsel to have been wrong in *every* statement they made. 21 Richard II., c. 1, is a Confirmation of Liberties in general, c. 6. "Item, The King, at the request of the said Commons, by the assent of the Lords of the Realm for the more surety of him and of his Realm in time to come, hath ordained and stablished that the issue Male of such persons forejudged now begotten shall not come to the Parliaments, nor to the Councils of the King, nor of his Heirs; saving always, that the Issue female of the said Persons forejudged and their Issues (which have strange fathers) shall not be indamaged by this statute" (c. 20). "Any one who attempts to repeal any of these Statutes shall be judged a traitor to the King and the realm." Now, at that time, as women generally acted by proxy, it proves that they had a *right to a representative.*

The second case, Chorlton *v.* Kessler, L. R., 4 C. P., p. 397, that of a woman freeholder at Rusholme with a county qualification with no relation to the 1832 Charter of Manchester, they refused to hear. Dr. Pankhurst was silenced. The Lord Chief-Justice said to him— "Do you expect to convince us that we are wrong, and that we ought to alter our judgment just given?" Dr. Pankhurst — "Your judgment is inchoate, and might be altered during the term. (Laughter.) This is not a point of Common Law but of Constitutional Law."

The next case was Wilson *v.* Town Clerk of Salford, L. R., 4 C. P., 398; Martha Wilson having appeared on the Overseer's List, and not having been objected to, wanted to know why she had been struck out. She was curtly referred to the decision in Chorlton *v.* Lings.*

The next case, Bennett *v.* Brumfitt, L. R., 4 C. P., 4070, was a consolidated appeal of men and women against the revising barrister at Ormskirk, who had held that certain notices of objection were valid, without the reasons of objection being stated. Here the Revising Barrister had decided that Ellen Ashcroft was qualified to vote. The Lord Chief-Justice interposed—"The Revising Barrister may have decided that Ellen Ashcroft had a right to vote, but we have decided that she has not." "But, your Lordship, what has to become of Birch, Roberts and the other men concerned in this appeal?" "It is laid down that where appeals are improperly consolidated they cannot be heard."

And thus, in a Court of Common Law, amid peals of irreverent laughter, the Constitutional Privilege of British Freewomen was *taken from them*, as a Justice worded it, "*for ever.*"

Yet Coke himself had declared "Judges ought not to give any opinion of a matter of Parliament because

---

* *See* the whole story in Miss Helen Blackburn's "History of Women's Suffrage," 1902.

it is not decided by the Common Law, but *secundum legem et consuetudinem* Parliamenti " (" Fourth Institute," 15).

In 1704, the Commons had resolved that "they cannot judge of the right of elections without determining the right of electors; and if the electors were at liberty to prosecute suits touching the right of giving voices in other courts, there might be different voices in other courts which would make confusion and be dishonourable to the House of Commons, and that such an action was a breach of privilege."

But this decison was accepted from the Common Law Courts, and, by Christmas, 1868, there was not a "Freewoman" left in Britain, except the *One* who sat on the throne, holding her privileges, not as her female subjects did, by Statutes written in general terms, but by Statutes where the language designates the male sex alone.

CHAPTER VIII

THE TURN OF THE TIDE

1868-1894

" Who would be free, themselves must strike the blow."—(BYRON.)

IT was not only the seven thousand women from Manchester and Salford who were disappointed in the results of their appeal. Women began on all sides to analyse the grounds of the judgment, and to take steps towards counteracting its baneful influence. An ever-increasing body of generous-hearted or far-seeing men joined their party, and worked with, and for them, both within and without the House of Commons. Meeting after meeting has spread enthusiasm. Petition after Petition has been presented. Bill after Bill has been brought forward. Amendment after Amendment has been proposed hitherto without success. As Mr. Stuart, M.P., once wittily said at a public meeting, "Petitions sent up by the Unrepresented, are like bell-handles rung outside of a door, that have no bell attached at the other end. They occupy the attention of those outside of the house, but do not disturb those that are within."

The strongest plea has been taken from women. By the extension of the Franchise in 1884, the Service Clause disallowed the doctrine that taxation was the qualification for representation, and reversed the prime reason of members being first called to the House in the reign of Hen. III. If women had felt it hard that their payment of taxes had not been sufficient to purchase their right of representation, they felt it harder that their payment of taxes, invalid and inoperative as regards themselves, was valid and operative as providing the qualification of their male servants, that, in short, the qualification had been altered fundamentally. Yet some good has come out of the evil. It has provided a *reductio ad absurdum*.

It has made women see clearly that no qualification, but that of sex, lies in the modern readings of the Statutes. They cannot alter the sex, but they may alter the Basis of Privilege. Such things have been done ere now. Ripe scholars in Mathematics have been excluded the Universities because they could not subscribe to the articles of the English Church. Political Economists have been excluded the House of Commons because they were of Jewish descent. These disabilities have been removed for men, and women have been admitted to the Universities. The political disabilities of sex must ere long be removed for women.

Progress has been very rapid since 1868. — The "woman's question" no longer provokes somnolence nor awakes mirth : it is treated as a question of gravity.

The publication of John Stuart Mill's "Subjection of Women," in 1869, educated many minds. The humorous treatment of the question in *Fraser's Magazine** in the article entitled, "Latest Intelligence from the Planet Venus," where logical objections against Male Enfranchisement are supposed to be urged by women, taught others that there were two sides to the principles of exclusion, and that those against the Enfranchisement of men, were, to say the least of it, quite as valid as any that have ever been brought against the Liberty of Women. Many other interesting volumes and articles have been written, making the views of women known.

Women have begun to speak for themselves, and to speak clearly—with no uncertain sound.

No new elucidation of the 1867 Charter has taken place except one very remarkable one. "If a woman's name were to get on an *election list by mistake*, and she afterwards tenders her vote, that vote must be accepted " ("Warren on Election Law," p. 175). (*See* also per Maule, Knapp and O., 415 (1835); per Rogers, Falc. and Fitz., 554 (1838), T. C. Anstey, 27.) The humour of the remark is great. As by the mistakes of some men women lost their rights, by a further masculine mistake they may regain them. Is this what it imports? If not, what?

The 1868 decision theoretically threw back civilisation 2000 years. But it necessitated opposition. One clear sign of this effect was given in 1869 when Mr. Jacob

* December, 1874.

Bright moved a resolution in the House that women should vote in Municipal affairs, and it was adopted almost without discussion. The Bill was modified, but reconfirmed in 1882.* The right has been exercised by women since that time without any overturning of the social fabric.

"At the Parliamentary Election of 1885, for the Borough of Camberwell, the returning officer of Camberwell refused to receive a paper nominating Miss Helen Taylor, the step-daughter of John Stuart Mill, as Parliamentary Candidate." (*See Law Journal*, 28th November, 1885.) Yet in 1887 the "Interpretations Act" confirmed Lord Brougham's reading of "woman" as "man."

In 1870 the vote for the School Boards, and eligibility thereto, were conferred upon women. Ancient rights allowed them to vote for Poor Law Guardians ; and in 1888 they were allowed to vote for County Councillors.† In 1894 they were made electors, and eligible for election on Parish and District Councils (56 and 57 Vict. c. 73, ss. 3 (2), 20, 23, 43).

Many Bills have been passed in their favour through the toil and energy of devoted women, and the co-operation of broad-minded men.

The Married Women's Property Acts of 1870 and of 1882 have secured the earnings of industrious wives from the clutches of grasping or drunken husbands to a

---

* Municipal Corporations (Elections) Act, 1869 (32 and 33 Vict. c. 55), s. 9 ; and Municipal Corporations Act, 1882 (45 and 46 Vict. c. 50), s. 63.

† *See* the County Electors Act, 1888 (51 Vict. c. 10), s. 2.

certain degree. A slight improvement has taken place in regard to the Custody of Infant Children. The Criminal Law Amendment Act of 1885 took a step in the right direction, though sadly crippled by its overriding conditions. (*See* Mrs. Fawcett's pamphlet on " The Criminal Law Amendment Act of 1885.")

Various other moral Bills have showed the woman's spirit working behind the scenes in favour of justice and mercy and chastity.

And the famous Clitheroe case, in 1891,* which sent back the Judge, through lack of Precedent, to the original Statutes to find a decision as to the imprisonment of a wife, bewildered the populace, and reduced the demand for wife-kicking boots.

Public Conscience is beginning to be awakened to the errors of its judgments in regard to women. The disproportionate awards of punishment to those who steal food when hungry, and those who maltreat their wives through tyranny, do not so often now arouse the indignation of those who read the Law Reports in newspapers.

Yet the tide has not been uniform in its motion. It is the way of waves to retire before and after a rise.

I forbear enlarging on the last great decision regarding women's disabilities, by which the Judge, following the example of his predecessor in Regina *v.* Chardstock, refused the electors of Brixton a right to elect Lady Sandhurst as County Councillor, and put another in her place that the majority of them had not

* Regina *v.* Jackson, L. R., 1891, 1 Q. B., 671 ; 64 L. T., 679.

elected; refused also to the County Councillors themselves their right of electing Miss Cons among their
Aldermen.   On 16th May, 1889, in the Queen's Bench
Division, was tried the case of Beresford-Hope *v.* Lady
Sandhurst (L. R. 23 Q. B. D. 79; 58 L. J. Q. B. 316;
61 L. T. R. 150).   The other candidates had given notice
of objections to the Lady, but the Returning Officer
disallowed these, studying only the Statute.   There were
1986 votes recorded in favour of Lady Sandhurst, and
1686 in favour of Beresford-Hope, who appealed.   It
was allowed, that the office being new, there was no
precedent to guide them; that the Municipal Corporations Act, 1882, had enacted that "for all purposes
connected with the right to vote at municipal elections,
words in this act importing the masculine gender include
women."   It was allowed that the Local Government
Acts of 1888 contain no enactments against women.

One Judge stated that it was a new office, but that no
woman had ever sat in a Municipal Corporation.   That
Anne Clifford was a *solitary* instance of a woman being
Sheriff.*   That it was necessary that a statute should
give express permission to women to be elected, because
Lord Brougham's Act does not apply to this.

Another Judge stated that his opinion would have
been in favour of the women's claim, but for the 63rd
Section of the Act of 1882.   But the majority of those
concerned, accepting the assertion " that a more learned
Judge never lived than Justice Willes," who had checked

* In this he was mistaken.   *See* ante., pp. 52-65.

the historical arguments in the case of Chorlton *v.* Lings
(L. R., 4 C. P., 374), accepted also the decision in that case
as the grounds of their ruling. " I take it, that neither
by the Common Law nor the Constitution of this country,
from the beginning of the Common Law until now, can
a woman be entitled to exercise *any* public function."
This book has been written to show the judges in error
in this statement.

One at least they forgot whom they might have
remembered, it was the Woman from whom they held
their Seals of office.

Thus Lady Sandhurst, after helping her colleagues,
her sex and her country, for a year, with two other brave
women, was turned out, and the Council and the Country
were alike the sufferers thereby. " Who will take care
of the Baby Farms, the Pauper Lunatic women, the
many small details that a man cannot know by accident,
and prides himself in not knowing by experience ? "
said that lady on her farewell to her colleagues.

If they have been defeated on the County Councils,
the success of women as Poor Law Guardians is
undeniable. The spirit of tenderness for those who
receive charity in their old age, the healing spirit of
sympathy for those that have been tempted ; the spirit
of exact investigation of accounts, and of economy in
expending the ratepayers' money, has certainly been
fostered by the presence of women on the Boards. The
same may be said of women on the School Boards.
They have offered themselves for many public appoint-

ments and offices. Sometimes they are accepted gladly; sometimes they are only not ejected because the law for doing so cannot be found.

A self-sacrificing worker in the cause of women has collected together and tabulated all the elections in which women might share all the public offices they might fill. (*See* "The Civil Rights of Women," by Mrs. Eva Maclaren. 1893.) Many of these were changed before Mrs. Elmy's "Report of the Women's Emancipation Union, 1899."

By the 31st December, 1906, women in England and Wales could be electors of *Municipal Councillors*, Municipal Corporations Act, 1882 (45 and 46 Vict. c. 50, s. 63); but in Regina *v.* Harrold (L. R., 7 Q. B., 361) it was decided that married women were not included; *County Councillors*, County Electors Act, 1888 (51 Vict. c. 10, s. 2), and Local Government Act, 1888 (51 and 52 Vict. c. 41, s. 2); *Urban District Councillors ; Rural District Councillors ; Poor Law Guardians ; Parish Councillors*, Married or Unmarried, Local Government Act, 1894 (56 and 57 Vict. c. 73, s. 43).

Women, married or unmarried, can be elected as *Urban District Councillors*, Local Government Act, 1894 (56 and 57 Vict. c. 73); *Rural District Councillors; Poor Law Guardians ; Parish Councillors*. They may be chairmen of these boards also, but if chairmen of Urban or Rural District Councils, they cannot be *ex officio* Justices of the Peace, as male chairmen would be. They can also be appointed by Co-option as *Members of Education Committees, and Managers of Public Schools*, Education Act, 1902 (2 Ed. VII., c. 42), and *Members of Distress Committees*, unemployed Workmen's Act, 1905 (5 Ed. VII., c. 18).

Nearly similar privileges are granted to women in Scotland and Ireland.

The "Qualifications of Women's Bill, 1907," again revolutionises every detail.

I take in a separate paragraph some questions regarding work and its returns, but it seems necessary first to show the advance of education during the period. I have always felt that our sex owes much to our late Queen Victoria simply for *being* what she was. At the time of the Reform Bill of 1832, she was being trained wisely for her future duties. The intellectual powers of a girl, when educated under favourable conditions, were brilliantly illustrated in her. The young Queen succeeded in 1837, and from the commencement of her reign there has been a constantly expanding view of the educatability even of ordinary girls. The want of good secondary schools was at first severely felt; but women began to patch up their education by private study or at public Lectures. The Philosophical Institution of Edinburgh, providing Lectures, Library, and Reading-Room, founded in 1846, was open from the first to women, as well as to men, and in many a large town were similar opportunities.

Mr. Thomas Oliphant of that city, in the same year,

started a large School in Charlotte Square, to which he added two "Advanced Classes" for the elder girls. There were taught Literature and Science in new and suggestive methods, that many women, still living, have rejoiced in. The Normal Schools for training Teachers had always been open to women; but these "Advanced Classes" were intended for women of leisure, those who had been accustomed to leave a Ladies' Finishing School, to become the Butterflies of Ball-Rooms, or better-class domestic drudges. A host of imitators showed the demand for schools of Mr. Oliphant's style.

In London, Queen's College, Harley Street, was founded in 1851; the Public Day School Company, since 1871, has done splendid work, and trained thousands of girls; and higher schools and colleges all over the country, have given solid education to a class of young women, to whom, formerly, the most superficial smattering was considered sufficient.

Meanwhile, the Secondary Education of women having succeeded, the higher education was attempted. The University Local Examinations, commenced for boys in 1858, were opened to girls in 1864, and to women as well as to men. They soon proved that they were able to take advantage of their opportunities. Strong efforts were made in many quarters to have them admitted to the Universities on equal terms with men. Failing this, there were strenuous attempts made to secure, at least, the education, if not the other privileges of a University career.

The earliest University Classes for Women were opened in Edinburgh in the winter of 1867-8, when 265 women enrolled themselves as students in Professor Masson's class on English Literature alone. In 1868-9, three branches of the Arts Curriculum were offered in Literature, Natural Philosophy, and Logic and Mental Philosophy ; opportunities which spread until the whole field was covered. In October, 1869, Hitchin Temporary College was opened for women in similar connection with Cambridge University. In 1873, the Oxford Association for the Education of Women took shape. In 1876, Glasgow and St. Andrews joined the work, and other opportunities all over the country had to be arranged to meet the ever-increasing demand.

The first University to grant degrees to women on equal terms was London, in the new Charter of 1878. As a non-teaching university, however, its gift of Degrees was limited by the opportunities opened to women of acquiring professional education in recognised colleges.

The Royal University of Ireland in Dublin opened in 1880, and in its original Charter granted equal terms for men and women ; and the Victoria University in 1880, allowing women instruction and examination in some departments, granted Degrees when they had passed sufficient examinations.

In 1892, the Scotch Universities were opened simultaneously.

All British Universities now admit women to education, and all to Degrees except Cambridge and Oxford.

Cambridge admits women to its education, its examinations, grants them a recognised place, but no Degrees. Oxford does this also, but also excludes them from full privileges. Dublin, however, now grants Degrees to those women educated in Oxford or Cambridge, who have taken honours, and London University Degrees are open to all.

In none of these Universities can women, even when on Convocation as Graduates, vote for the University Member of Parliament. The same anomaly exists as holds in relation to women having a property qualification. The meaning of words is changed. The real qualification in a University is based upon attending certain classes, passing certain examinations, living under certain conditions, and paying certain fees. Women fulfil all these duties, but they must not, even from their Alma Mater, however willing they may be, receive the same privilege as their brothers, on a University Qualification ; because the Reform Bill of 1867, while granting the franchise to all men on a property qualification, by clause 5, limited it to "male persons in Universities." It is possible that, after a little more of the Higher Education, it will be found that they have attained "an improved understanding," enough to allow them even to vote by the side of the navvy and the pot-boy.

The many years past have not been lost, however, even in regard to Women's Suffrage. Meanwhile have been growing up young men and young women, educated under the broadening effect of more equal privileges in learning. The old restrictions seem to them meaningless in the new light of reason. A generous youth, in the older Universities, who has been beaten by a woman in a mathematical examination, must feel his brow flush when he receives the reward that is denied to her, and feel shame instead of pride that he has to be protected against her competition. He would never dream of suggesting that she would "require an improved understanding to vote for a Parliament man" if she can attain First-Class Honours. In the youth of the country lies hope, if the youth be but trained aright.

The result of the educational opportunities has been to give women personal capability of entering professional life. But the Professions have certain powers of excluding competitors, and they have all done what they could to make entrance difficult or impossible. Women are now admitted to the Medical Profession. Several original professions they have invented for themselves, and they have done their best with the old. They have therefore gained new powers of acquiring property. Their energy and self-dependence have revolutionised the thoughts of men as regards their capability, and any objection on that ground now must be disingenuous or prejudiced.

John Stuart Mill, in his "Subjection of Women," p. 99, says: "If anything conclusive can be inferred from experience, without psychological analysis, it would be that the things women have not been allowed to do are just those that they succeed best in doing." Association of ideas is doing its work in forming customs and in moulding habits of thought. No longer is a woman an incongruous sight in Halls of Learning or of Research, in Scientific Societies or on Boards of Guardians. Those who exclude women are learning that they themselves suffer by the exclusion.

They welcome them eagerly as Canvassers at elections. Ere long they will find it both natural and desirable to invite them to co-operate with them through the Ballot-box, " to choose a Knight of the Shire or a Burgess from a Borough, in the stead of all and of each of them, to go to the Parliament House, and there, consulting with the Knights of other Shires," to defend the interests of *those who sent them.*

CHAPTER IX

OTHER WOMEN

"All sisters are *co-parceners* one with another. The elder-born has no privilege over the younger."

IF in these pages I have not noted the great majority of women who never have had, under any condition, any privilege of any kind, it is not because I have forgotten them. The needle-workers, whose toil is doubled and whose pay is halved by self-enriching sweaters; the labouring women, toiling in unfavourable conditions alongside of men now privileged with voices powerful enough to control their earnings; the tempted women, whose temptations are made strong and dangerous for them through false social and economic views; the poor married women, who may be happy only according to the degree that their husbands are better than the Law allows them to be; the poor mothers to whom Slave Law is still applied in regard to their children. But the principles of Method lead us to take one step at a time; the doctrines of Logic prevent us confusing two ideas; and the Precedents of the Law Courts teach us that "where claims are improperly consolidated they cannot

be heard" (*see* Bennett *v.* Brumfitt, L. R., 4 C. P.,
407, ante., p. 175, 1868).

To lose the possible reward of any effort by
misplacing it, is, to say the least of it, unwise.

Men have placed all women in one class now. We
are all sisters, and "co-parceners" one with another.
They have extended political privileges to all, under
conditions very easy to fulfil, except to Aliens, Minors,
Lunatics, Criminals, and *Women*. The Alien may
become naturalised, the Minor may attain majority,
the Lunatic may regain his reason and may even vote
in a *lucid interval*, and when a Criminal has served his
time, he may become once more a *free British Elector*.
The noblest and the best, the most learned and philanthropic of women, classed with the worst, are reckoned
as something lower than the lowest Criminal. He may,
combining with others of his class, urge on his narrow,
selfish views ; they may not enrich the world by advancing the high, generous ideals that lie nearest their
hearts. If any women, on any qualification, become
enfranchised, the disability of sex-in-itself will be
removed, and to all others thereby will be given a
ray of hope. It has seemed to me through following
a Psychological study of the springs of human action,
that the class most likely to receive Enfranchisement
first, is that which formerly had it. Therefore I, with
others who would not be immediately concerned in
the success of our efforts, join hands in toil to help
forward the claims of those who have been British

Freewomen, as that section of the community which can claim most on Historical grounds and by Legal Precedents. We hope that they, being given the chance, will help their less fortunate sisters.

We must not forget, that the very Charters that have so mightily multiplied the legions of *Freemen in Esse*, have likewise increased the number of *Freewomen in Posse*

M. Talleyrand Perigord,* once Bishop of Autun, observes "that to see one half of the human race excluded by the other, from all participation in Government, is a political phenomenon that on abstract principles it is impossible to explain." We think the phenomenon very capable of explanation, but the reason is to be found, not in the perfection of human nature, but in its incompleteness.

When the light increases, so that men can see to read aright, then women may be able "to take up their Freedom too."

The Romance of the old world was carried on by the "fair women and brave men," little being said of the *plain women* and the *weak men*. Civilisation has advanced far enough to recognise the claims of the *weak men*; we want it to go further, and help wisely the cause of the *weak women*. For that we require, reversing the adjectives, armies of "brave women and fair men," *brave women* who seek not their lost birthright with

* *See* Dedication of Mary Wollstonecraft's "Vindication of the Rights of Women."

N

futile tears, but with self-sacrificing energies and heart-inspired sympathies ; and *fair men* who can understand that none lose through another's gain, and that theirs is not Liberty but License, that use a self-asserted power to the restriction of the rights and privileges of others.

Various tests have been proposed to mark different degrees of Civilisation. I believe that the commonplace man of to-day might suggest that the multiplication of Machinery is the most satisfactory index. More thoughtful men would consider a recognition of the first principles of Justice a safer ground. Some of these assert that the position of women is the surest test of the Civilisation of a Country and of a Time. If this be so, nineteenth century men must look to their character as posterity will judge it, for the century is very near its close. They are apt to be judged not by what they have done, but by what they have left undone.*

In reality one cause of the existence of so much statutory evil is this, that the majority of men are so much better than the laws—they do not understand their full bearing.

Victor Hugo has said, " Man was the problem of the eighteenth century, Woman is the problem of the nine-teenth." To understand and solve that problem, a totally different set of reasonings must be applied than have hitherto been used by the majority of men. The

* I have left this statement as it stood. We know now that nineteenth century men have been *weighed and found wanting*. It ought to be a caution to twentieth century men to reform their ways speedily.

so-called " Physical Force Argument " is, after all, but
the ghost of a Dead Argument raised to scare the timid
in the night. It can be valid only in Savage times, when
Might makes Right. It is inoperative in Civilisations,
where Justice even *pretends* to decide the rights of men.
Even under the "physical force argument," some women
might be free. Many women are stronger than many
men ; and many women have been known to signalise
that strength, not only in disguise as soldiers, or as
navvies, but openly, fearless, and free. Their physical
strength has been shown by many brilliant examples,
as well as by their exercise of certain trades.* The
courage of Nicholaa de la Haye and Black Agnes of
Dunbar ; of the Countess of Derby and the Marchioness
of Hamilton during the Civil War has been emulated by
many others.

" The Lord Marquis of Hamilton's mother commands
a regiment, and led them into Edinburgh with a case
of pistols at her saddle and a case at her side. Our
ladies are not more skilful in curling and poudringe
than the Scotchwomen in charging and discharging
their pistols." (Letter from Sir Henry Herbert,
Edinburgh, June, 1639. Letters of the Herbert

---

* In Somerset, "One of the ferdell-holders (*i.e.*, holder of a
quarter of a virgate of land) found all the Blacksmith's work for the
Lord's horses and ploughs, and at the time of the compilation of the
Custumal of Bleadon in the thirteenth century," this RENT for her
land was paid by the widow Alicia as Common Smith of the Vill or
Manor. ("Papers on the Custumal of Bleadon, as illustrative of
the History and Antiquities of Wilts," 1857, p. 193.)

Family.) We know that a large number of women desired to form a Volunteer Regiment lately, but were refused permission by the authorities.

Some men assert scornfully that women are not fit for privilege or power. To assert a thing is not to prove it. If women are not fit for the Franchise, perhaps it may be made fit for them. It is perfectly certain that they are fitted to enjoy justice and to benefit by freedom.

Some sentimentalists say that women are too pliable and delicate to be exposed to the roughnesses of political life. It would destroy their charm. To such objectors I would answer, Look out into the flat meadows where sluggish streamlets wind, and see in the inartistic clumps of pollard-willows an illustration of the manner in which "woman's nature" has been treated by such men. Though their roots and leaves are the same, though their upward aspirations are permanent, and their vital energies restorative, yet through top-pruning at the will of others, for the use of others, the growth and the ideals of the trees have been marred for ever. Nothing can ever restore to a Pollard-Willow its natural place in the picture-gallery of trees. But its distortion has only been individual, its offspring through freedom may develop into a perfect tree, really sweet and graceful, and not artificially so.

Other sentimentalists say that women are angels, and their purity must not be contaminated by contact with the great outer world of vile realities. They mistake fragile butterflies for God's Angels. These are spirits strong in His strength, whose inward purity gives them power to pass unscathed through external impurity, whose sympathy gives them knowledge, and whose presence purifies and refines the moral atmosphere. The more a woman is like an Angel the more is she needed to counsel and to work with men.

That women do not want it, is another futile objection. No classes or masses ever unanimously want saving regeneration of any kind, until the few have made it seem desirable to them. We know that at least over a quarter of a million women in this country do want it, and have set their hands to the great "Appeal to the Members of Parliament" to grant them political freedom for weighty reasons. To refuse that quarter million what the other millions do not ask, is like refusing to the Eagle and the Lark the right to fly, because the Ostrich and the Swan do not care for the exercise.

Others boldly say that this is a man's world, and in it men must rule. It is true that man has long led in the Song of Life, with words and music written at his will, and women has but played an Accompaniment. Sometimes in their Duets she has been forced to sing a shrill second or a piping Bass, in notes that have no meaning when they are sung alone. But he did not see or hear, and she dared not say, that this was not the sole part that she could sing or play. In the many-voiced Concert of the Universe, where harmonious "parts" should combine in balanced perfection, there are constant discords and recurrent "clangs," because man has misunderstood the Rules of Harmony. The bass voices are necessary for perfection, but too much bass becomes monotonous to the listening ear, and overpowering the finer notes, spoils the conception of the whole. If there is anything in this analogy, it is the woman's voice that should lead the melody and express the meaning, and the man's voice should support her notes and enrich the harmony. One need not analyse the various other objections. None of them are based on Truth, Justice, Logic, or History.

In my second Chapter I spoke somewhat of women's privilege as heiresses, but I would like here to add a few words about unprivileged earners.

Labour is the Basis of Property.—I do not wish now to analyse all the Economic Theories regarding the relations of Property to Labour, but only the one that touches our question. In olden times Labour was paid in kind. Money is an arbitrary sign of possession, and possession is a sign of labour, as speech is of thought. Money is an easy medium by which the returns of labour can be transferred, either in purchase of other property or of other labour, or as a free gift or inheritance.

In ancient times fighting was considered a kind of labour, the highest kind. The Service of the King was the most honourable, save that of the Service of the Church. Fighting and praying were alike paid in land or in coin, and the land or the coin could be inherited by those who neither fought nor prayed. Hard-working traders and farmers also earned coin and land, and sometimes left their gains to idle children. Hence owners have not always been earners. Some writers on National Economy have inveighed against the principle of inheritance. To me it seems natural and right that what a man has produced by labour, he may leave to his descendants, at least, when he does so by old Saxon Law. There has been much virulent denunciation of Landlords, especially in relation to the *unearned increment of property* in thriving towns. I do not know any, however, who have discussed a question, that bears much upon the Argument of this book.*

The Unrecorded Increment of Woman's Labour.— Earners are not always owners. Except where a woman brought some fortune at her marriage it has been supposed that her husband "supported her." But in the majority of respectable middle-class or workmen's dwellings this is very far from being the case.

The woman labours as well as her husband. If property is the result of labour, both can be expressed in figures. Let us take the case of a man earning 30s. a week for eight hours' work a day, and five hours on Saturday, forty-five in all. The payment for each hour is 8d. As the woman spends no time walking to and from her work; as she has no rest on Saturdays or Sundays except through extra work on other days; as she on these other days works very many more hours than

* It has, however, been treated by others since this passage was written.

her husband, she has bettered the common stock by the amount of ninety hours of work ; which taken at half the wage, rises to the same sum, so that the common income should be reckoned at 60s. instead of 30s. But her share being received in kind, it is unrecognised and unrecorded. This may be made clear by supposing that some other person had fulfilled the wife's duties. In transferring flour into bread she earns what the baker otherwise would gain in the difference between flour and the price of the loaf. In washing and ironing the family linen she earns what the laundress would charge for the same, minus the cost of soap and coals. In carrying a heavy basket from the distant stores, she earns what the local grocer would have done in the difference between wholesale and retail prices ; in making clothes for her children out of her own frayed garments, she earns what the draper would have charged for similar material, and what the dressmaker would have required for making it up. If she patches her husband's clothes, she earns the tailor's charge. Her daily scrubbing and cooking may be reckoned at charwoman's wages, and thus, multiplied by the hours of labour, the proportion may come out. Both she and her husband dimly feel that she has saved expenditure, they never realise that she has acquired property.

The spending also must be reckoned. The result of the man's labour has been translated into coin, a more convenient form in which to pay rent and taxes, the Club-money, and direct shop-purchases for both. Of the common diet the man has the larger and better share. Beyond this he generally has a daily paper, a pipe and beer. At the lowest estimation these cost 3s. 6d. a week. If he has no vices, there may be 3s. in his pocket at the end of the week, and that 3s. may be put into a Savings Bank in his name, which, after years of saving, *by modern* law, he may will away from his wife and children.

What of her toil, her earnings, her increment of property? It has seemed to vanish, but it has really enriched him. This may easily be seen if, leaving her domestic employments, she goes out to labour as charwoman in the house of others at 2s. 6d. a day of ten hours. She there also receives food. The position then is this. The common house-property is increased by the expenditure on her food being saved. She still saves somewhat to her family in comfort and money by working overtime. Her husband has either to do without some of his comforts or her economies, or spend some hours of his relaxation in home-work. But at the end of the week, there is the visible increment of 15s. shillings. Before 1870 all that belonged legally to the husband, since that time it belongs nominally to the wife. That is the meaning of the Married Women's Property Bill. A husband should support a wife, but the money she earns she may keep to herself. But it is hard on wives and mothers that their share in the common property should be unrecognised when their toil is continued under the ordinary domestic conditions; but be recognised when circumstances or inclination make it possible for them to seek a visible money reward elsewhere.

We will take another example from a higher rank. Suppose a man has £300 a year, and is left a widower with four young children, he at once feels the diminution of his income, through the increase of his needs. He must have a housekeeper, at a salary, at least, of £25. Her keep costs him another £30. He must find a daily governess to teach the children, and walk with them. Without keep that may cost another £25. He has to pay the dressmaker for making and repairing the children's clothes, at least £10. He has to pay workmen to hang pictures, put up curtains, to paint the back-garden fence, or enamel the nursery bath; to cover the drawing-room chairs, or patch the dining-room sofa, quite £10 a year. His wife's whole keep had been saved through greater care in purchasing and managing food, and higher skill in cooking than either his housekeeper or assistant-girl possesses; and the man has not only lost the love and comfort of his wife, but the £100 a year which she indirectly earned for him. He thought his income was £300, and was all his own; he finds it had really been £400, as compared to the present receipts of expenditure, and that the missing £100 had been earned by her. He would have found this out had he allowed her to give music-lessons as she wished to do, a light labour that she loved. Or she might have written that weekly letter to the country paper she was asked to do. She might have earned £100 a year at that, and that money would have been *her own* to spend in luxury or charity if she pleased, or to have saved up for her children's future. But then his tradesmen's bills would have been increased. It is absurd, therefore, to believe that a wife's earnings are limited to those hours that she takes from her husband's service and sells to some other employer of labour, who pays her in so much coin of the realm.

But the *partner* that touches the coin seems always to take the lead. We may see this in the circumstances where the positions are altered, as, for instance, among many fishing communities. There, though the men go out at night and fish, the women not only do their domestic work, but receive the fish, go out and sell it, make the necessary purchases, and "bank" the remainder of the money. The superior intelligence and relative social position of the women in fishing communities has often been noted. I have heard it scornfully said of a fisher-girl, "She marry? Why, she is not able to keep a man!" In this illustrative case, the woman holds the purse, and her share in the family earnings is recognised.

Now, if privilege is based on property, and property is based on labour, how is an industrious woman shut out from the benefits of both? Why must the man only have the earner's vote? One vivifying revelation of our half-century is the recognition of the nobility of labour. No one has so gracefully expressed it as Mrs. Barret

Browning in "Aurora Leigh," when, urging all to work, she adds:

> "Get leave to work;
> In this world 'tis the best you get at all,
> For God in cursing, gives us better gifts
> Than man in benediction."

But even with her it was too much *work for its own sake*. It has taken fuller education, even since her time, for women to recognise that it is equally noble and just for them to receive the reward of toil in earning as it is for a man; and to be able to keep or use these earnings as they will. A century ago, men suffered somewhat from the state of things they had themselves initiated. An eldest son that received all the inheritance and privilege had therewith to support the women of his father's family as well as of his own. It was disgraceful for him as well as for them that they should *earn money*. But they gave him labour, acting as upper servants, butts of ridicule, as the case might be, or blind worshippers when all the outer world had learned to disbelieve in him. Their recreation was the manufacture of useless Berlin-wool monstrosities; or self-sacrificing work in pauperising the poor of the parish, under the misdirection perhaps of an inexperienced curate. Higher education was discredited; literary aspiration a shamefaced secret. Miss Austin had to hide her pen and ink and manuscripts by a piece of fancy-work kept handy, lest her world should know and speak its mind of her and her dreadful doings. The only profession open to a lady was matrimony; and the chances of happy matrimony were thereby enormously decreased.

If the dignity of being able to earn money has raised women immensely in social life, their higher education has made this earning possible. Dependent sisters need no longer hang their heads in shame before supporting brothers. If they are not needed in their homes, they may go forth into the world, eat the sweet bread of honest labour, and become *individuals*.

But the woman is fettered still by the trammels of custom, by the protection accorded to males; by false social and economic creeds which teach that man's work must be paid higher than woman's, whether it is better done or not; by man's power of place, which gives him power of veto; by inherited thought-fallacies and linguistic inaccuracies; by the nature of the medium through which things are seen.

Bacon wisely advised men to study all things in the "lumen siccum" or dry light of science, lest vapours arising from the mind should obscure the vision. He also pointed out that "There are four classes of Idols which beset men's mind. To these for distinction sake I have assigned names—calling the first class Idols of the Tribe; the second, Idols of the Cave; the third, Idols of the Market-place; the fourth, Idols of the Theatre" ("Novum Organum," Article xxxix., p. 53; also in lix.). "But the Idols of the Market-place are the most troublesome of all; idols which have crept into the understanding through the alliances of words and names. For men believe that their reason governs words; but it is also true that words react on the understanding." Such a confusion I find in the use of the word "Man." Is it a common or masculine term? It was a common noun in the days when women could be *freemen;* in the nineteenth century it has become a hybrid, the lawyers having decided for us that the word "Man" includes "woman" when a penalty is imposed, and never includes woman when a privilege is conferred. But even when that distinction is made clear, that other distinction between the represented and the unrepresented is the foundation of much evil.

After an impartial analysis of the laws regarding women, can men say that they are just? Can they continue to assert that they know better than women do what they need, and wish, and strain after; and if they know, will they *do* the thing that is necessary? With the best will in the world, which I believe the majority of men have, they do not know how. Only the foot that wears the shoe knows just where it pinches, and feels keenly the need of alteration.

Why must a woman be unable to free herself from an unfaithful husband if his hand is restrained from personal cruelty?

Why may a noble and loving mother have less power over the children she bore, and toiled for, than a selfish, indifferent father, who still "has sacred rights, because he has sacred duties" that he has despised?

Why must strong men inherit their father's unwilled property before weak women?

Why must a bad workman be paid higher wages than a good workwoman?

Why are all laws in regard to vice notoriously unequal?

Why have labouring men the right injuriously to determine the conditions and opportunities of the labour of women working by their side?

It is because men are represented in Parliament and women are not.

"The House of Commons is as sensitive to the claims of the Represented as the mercury is to the weather." If women, oppressed by various burdens, wish their will should reach the House, they must be given a voice. The only method by which the needs and wishes of women can be considered duly is by classing them once more among the "represented." In vain otherwise will they look to their friends in the House to help various Bills they desire to pass, or to restrain other Bills they desire not to pass. It is not their friends they require to affect, it is their opponents. And their opponents can only be converted to the woman's cause when women become Electors. That Bills affecting the liberties of more than half of the whole population should be left in the hands of "private members," that they should be left to the chance of a private members' ballot, that a Machinery Bill, or any other Bill affecting the interests of the smallest class of Electors, should be allowed to "talk out" the limited time allowed for the discussion of a question of such magnitude, shows the peculiar and sinister aspect in which Bills affecting the "unrepresented" can be viewed.

Archimedes of old said that he could move the world if he had but a " place where to stand." If women want to move their world, to affect its destinies and their own, they too must have a place where to stand, and the place where to stand is the Suffrage.

" I trust the suffrage will be extended on good old English principles, and in conformity with good old English notions of representation" (" Essay on the Constitution," by Lord Russell).

What these were I have attempted to show.

Apart from the special measures urgently needed on behalf of women, most public measures affect them equally with men.

A woman grocer is as much interested in Sugar Bounties and in Tea-taxes as her male rivals.

A woman housekeeper needs as much to be protected against the imposition of frozen home or foreign meat, at fresh English prices, as does the burdened British farmer.

All women suffer as much in War, and gain as much by Peace as men do.

Noxious trades, impure air, bad drainage, poison women as they do men. Women have as much interest in the character and wisdom of the members of the house as men have, because they also suffer from the consequences of their unwise actions. How, therefore, can anyone say—these things do not concern women?

It would be better for men too if women were represented. They would then understand, for the first time, the meaning of Justice, and enjoy in return the blessings of fair-play. They would discover that in the very difference of women lies one great argument for their being consulted.

If public-spirited women continue to be denied the power of offering their judgment in the consensus of public opinion on political matters, the nation will be the poorer. It will ere long recognise this. But it does not yet.

How can any Assembly be said to be "Representative of the People," when the best half of the People are not represented there; the best half in numbers, through the working out of the modern doctrine of the Survival of the Fittest, more boys are born than girls, more women are alive than men; the best half by Statistics, as there are five times as many male criminals as female; the best half in Economics, as in spite of all their disadvantages there are fewer female paupers than male paupers; the best half, by the position in which God placed woman at the Creation, at the Fall, and the Redemption.

There is a strange suggestive duality even in our physical frame. We have two eyes, two ears, two hands, two feet, many other dualities, and two lobes of the brain to control them. If by any cause one lobe of the brain is injured, it is the *other side* of the body that becomes paralysed, but the whole body suffers with its members. If men persist in using only one eye, they not only see things out of focus, but restrict their range of vision. They can only see things on the near side of them. A Government that only uses the masculine eye, and sees but the masculine side of things, is at best but a *one-eyed* Government. The builder that only toils with one hand impoverishes himself, and makes meaner the design of the great Architect. The traveller that through some brain-sick fancy imagines one of his feet to be decrepit, can get along but by hops and jerks, or by using crutches made of dead wood, instead of living limbs that make motion graceful, equal, and rapid. Yet thus men do, wondering, meanwhile, that the "times are out of joint."

Let them apply reason to their time-worn aphorisms, and the scales of justice to their out-worn Customs. Let them look at Humanity as it is, and as it ought to be.

Two comparisons will help them in the review, their comparison with their ancestors in this respect, and their comparison with "the perfect man in Christ Jesus," and His "perfect Law of Liberty."

For Revelation has enriched our education. Through much misconstruction and misconception the vision of Creation has been coloured by the prejudice of men.

God made man in His own image, male and female; man has made him altogether male. The Creator said, "It is not good for man to be alone." His creature asserts, "It is best for us to be alone." But it never has

been good; it is not good now. Only in following out
the lines of God's conception can *man* (*homo*) remain in
the image of God. Early names were all connotative,
recording some special quality or association, and the
early name of Adam was "Dust," and the meaning of
Eve is "Life." The Titanic and Earth-born Physical
force of which Adam was made the representative, must
be united to that which *lives and brings Life*, to make
one perfect being. Only through the spiritual and
practical union of Man with Woman can society be
regenerated. When Woman ate of the Tree of the
knowledge of Good and Evil, she learned more clearly
to distinguish the good from the evil and to chose that
good. Therefore, God chose the Woman as His fellow-
worker in the scheme of Redemption. As part of the
curse of Satan it is part of the primeval blessing of
Humanity, that "I will put enmity between thee and the
Woman." The hands that restrict the Woman's power,
and limit her opportunity of fulfilling her mission, are
fighting against God's Will.

The words of God, "Thy desire shall be unto thy
husband, and he shall rule over thee," is a prophecy
of man's wrong and not a statute of man's right. To
understand this we have only to collate the passage with
that other in which God speaks to Cain before he slew
his brother—"If thou doest well shalt thou not be
accepted, and if thou doest not well sin lieth at the door.
And unto thee shall be his desire, and thou shalt rule
over him."

The result of the first "physical force argument" was the death of the "righteous Abel." The result of the same argument, through centuries of human existence, has been the death-in-life of the Woman whom God opposed to Satan. And the paralysis of the half has affected the whole body, Social and Politic.

The Divine and Human are united through the Woman.

It is only by the representative Woman that Christ becomes the "Son of Man."

Christ, as His Father did, took women to be His friends and fellow-workers. Women never forsook Him. Women watched by His cradle and spread the "glad tidings" ere yet He had opened His lips. Simeon rejoiced that his own eyes had seen God's Salvation, but the prophetess Anna was the first preacher of Christ. Fearless women stood by His Cross and saw the last of His life; faithful women went to the Tomb, learned first of His Resurrection, and were made His messengers to the Apostles.

Through the ages, the contest between Satan and the Woman, and between the Seed of Satan and the Seed of Woman, has been made unduly hard both for Man and Woman, because of the Woman being bound both hand and foot. "The Dragon was wroth with the Woman and went to make war with the Remnant of her Seed which keep the Commandments of God, and have the Testimony of Jesus Christ" (Rev. xii. 17).

Let her have Freedom and Fair Play. Let her show

what, God helping her, she can do, when men cease hindering her in the development of *Herself.* They also will be gainers thereby. How can men be their own possible best as long as they connive at the oppression of women? It will seem a new Creation when the earlier-born *Freeman* meets the later-born *Freewoman* and recognises at last that it was not good for him to have been so long alone. For any Moral Regeneration, or for any Political Stability, men must learn to distinguish Good from Evil, Justice from short-sighted Selfishness, and to see, in the recognition of Woman as a helpmeet for them *in all things*, the fulfilment of God's Will in regard to both.

The Truth shall make you *Free !*

CHAPTER X

CONCLUSION

" Every presumption is to be made in favour of Liberty (in favorem Libertatis)." Legal Maxim (*see* "Encyclopædia of the Laws of England," vi., 424.)

DURING the thirteen years which have elapsed since the first edition of this book was written, women have done many things : they have made discoveries, patented new inventions, written great books, conducted good magazines, painted fine pictures, given popular lectures, healed diseases, taught schools and colleges with brilliant success ; the greatest woman in the land has completed her glorious reign with an unparalleled length of years, and an unbroken record of political insight; but they have not yet attained the vote, not even in the Universities, though occasionally they have come out there head and shoulders above any of their male competitors, and so frequently side by side that intellect has been proved to be of no sex. No one again dare say honestly that a woman would "require an improved intelligence to vote for a member of Parliament."

Neither can any opponent say, intelligently, that

" Women do not want the vote." As soon as a woman learns to understand what it means, she wants it ; and they are all being educated gradually to know what it means by earnest women preachers, and by those stern teachers—the cruel pressure of circumstances under unjust laws. They have toiled and spent themselves and their money freely, some of them have even spent their lives. No cause that has ever yet been fought in the country has cost so much, no cause has ever had so many petitions sent up in its support. But it is just because they are not electors that their efforts and their petitions have so little power. " The Great Appeal " from women of all parties and all classes, which was finally presented to the House of Commons in 1596, numbered 257,796 signatures. Yet it was cast aside and forgotten so far, that this season it was omitted from the reckoning of the numbers of the sum total of women who wanted the vote. No man can ever again say that women are incapable of wide-spread organised work for the public good. Miss Flora Stevenson, the sole member of the Edinburgh School Board, who was returned at every election, and who was chairman of the Board for years before her death ; Miss Beale, who had raised Cheltenham College to its high place among schools, were openly named at the great public Demonstration in the Queen's Hall, by Sir Wilfrid Lawson, as the greatest organisers in the country. And they have had many worthy peers on School Boards, Vestries, Boards of Guardians, in Schools and Colleges, in numerous societies for the good of others; but they are still denied the power to work out their mission fruitfully, the power to express *themselves*, which is allowed to every pot-boy, gambler, drunkard, if he be a man.

The exclusion is of itself the most convincing proof of their urgent need of the protection of the vote. How can men who deny justice to women be fit to understand or to legislate for their needs?

This has at last dawned even upon the most optimistic women. There are Women's Suffrage Societies in all the great towns of the country, and in many of the smaller ones. These have become combined in the "National Union of Women's Suffrage Societies," with a Council and an Executive, to secure unity in its great efforts. Many of the Women's Societies, instituted for other ends, have come to see that it is necessary to make women's suffrage a part of their creed, such as "The British Women's Temperance Association," "The Lancashire and Cheshire Women's Textile Union," "The Women's Co-operative Union," "The Nurses Registration Society," many political associations, and most charitable associations; indeed, nearly all of those that combine to make the National Union of Women workers for the common good. The greatest new Society, the Women's Social and Political Union, has recognised that nothing can be done for the betterment of humanity until women are enfranchised.

What have we all done through the last thirteen years?

We have had the *great appeal* sent in, the appeal in which 3,500 women, in 1894, had helped to collect names to the number of 257,796; but as no Bill was brought forward which it might back, during 1894 and 1895, it was delayed until 1896, when the volumes in which the signatures had been classified, constituency by constituency, occupied the long tables in Westminster Hall, past the Statue of Queen Mary to that of James I. It was intended to support the Bill, which stood, in the name of Mr. Faithfull Begg, first on the orders of the day for 20th May of that year. Little result came of all our work, but deepened enthusiasm in the heart of the workers. An enthusiastic gathering took place in the Queen's Hall to greet the Delegates from the National Council of Women in the United States, and nine other countries, when the great quinquennial Conference was held in London, June and July, 1899.

Petition after petition has been sent up, one from 29,000 women of the Lancashire factories was personally conveyed by a deputation of fifteen working women, escorted by Miss Roper, and placed in the hands of a group of friendly members in a committee-room in the House on 18th October, 1901. It was only a sign how the working women had come to learn that it was a question of bread and butter to them, and of an honest life. Side by side with this petitioning went on the constant spade-work, the constant sowing, the constant reaping in the harvest of those awakened to the urgent need of the vote. Conference after conference has been held with Parliamentary committees of friends to the cause, as to the best methods of procedure. Work at all bye-elections is now recognised to be *only done* for candidates friendly to the cause; work at the last General Election brought in an unprecedented majority of members pledged to vote for Women's Suffrage. With high hopes we believed that our long-looked-for opportunity had come. Taunted by the unbelieving that " Women did not want the Vote," we welcomed and signed Miss Clementina Black's simple declaration : "I desire to have the Parliamentary Franchise on the same terms as it is, or may be, granted to men."

Some women, it is true, started an antagonistic declaration, but it has not done us much harm, though it has justified our opponents in their own eyes. We have even humbled ourselves to the dust, and walked in a damp February day through muddy streets, in a procession two miles long, from Hyde Park Corner to Exeter Hall, with our banners in our hands, and our rosettes of red and white upon our breast—a procession that wanted not employment, but justice and freedom ; a procession educating to many who saw, and to more, a sign of a determination that *must* be yielded to. I heard a 'bus-driver's appeal to a mounted policeman : " Give them the vote, but don't let them stop the traffic ! " At Exeter Hall, on the arrival of the processioners there was a stirring meeting.

We had had deputation after deputation, nothing came to anything ; then the lead passed out of our hands to those

of the Women's Social and Political Union, who, seeing
the failure of our peaceful and legitimate methods, made
a new departure, and became, as they call themselves,
" practical politicians." Recognising that "the Government is a machine which can only work under pressure,
they have applied that pressure. They have attended
men's political meetings ; they have held great meetings
of their own in great halls and in the open air; they
have carried unanimous resolutions of the urgency of
attending to the wants of women ; they have attempted
to hand these resolutions to the Prime Minister himself,
so that there might be no mistake that it had reached
him. But their measures landed many of them in
prison (143 in all), and brought some to the very gates
of death. The martyr spirit is in the air, such as has
breathed into the souls of all who have at any time
worked for freedom. They are working at every bye-
election against the nominees of the very Government
on which they build their hopes, that they might give it
the necessary sense of pressure to make it move. The
stirring enthusiasm of their members provides them with
funds for all they wish to do. They have moved the
Press to find interest and even sensationalism in their
doings. Nothing more clearly marks the change in the
attitude of the external world to our cause than the fact
that thirteen years ago, women Suffragists took small
halls, and if they had very good speakers they would
have a fair audience, and a short paragraph appeared
about their doings in some of the papers. Now, they

can take the largest halls in the city, charge concert prices, fill it full to overflowing, and then have the courage to ask for a collection, and the *savoir faire* to get it, not in little driblets, but in sums that rise to four figures, and the Press makes head-lines of their columns. Plays pourtraying their aims and actions have filled theatres, two of them at a time, and plays, too, that did not beat about the bush, but talked of nothing else than the " Votes for Women."

There is one good that has come to women through their long journey of forty years through the Wilderness, since John Stuart Mill's Trumpet-Call to Freedom, and the Representation of the People's Act of 1867 became law in terms that gave them the statutory right to the vote through the application of Lord Brougham's Act. If they have not reached the Promised Land, they can see it clearly ahead, and *they know the way to get there*. They have recognised the power of combination, the meaning of solidarity and unity. Their common wrongs have levelled all class distinctions, all intellectual inequalities, all religious differences. Men have made justice a sex prerogative ; women are determined it shall be shed upon all ; men have kept freedom to themselves ; women have determined to break their shackles, for, without that, they cannot do their duty to God, their country, or themselves. Therefore, all who really want this great fundamental reform have agreed to give up all minor aims, and to seek that " place where to stand," whence alone they can act upon anything with power and permanency.

What have men been doing for us the while? Many of them, all of them who have either a fine sense of justice or generosity, have become enthusiastic fellow-workers with us for the common good; many of them who have not awaked to enthusiasm, but have a sense of Logic and a Knowledge of History, have been constrained to acknowledge " if you want a vote, there is no reason you should not have it," others still dwell in molluscous indifference to the stories of sweated women and suffering children; and others, through various obscure causes, have been stirred to a feeling of rancour and animosity at our modest demands, and have exerted themselves actively against us. Some of these, with that curiously illogical method by which they deal with the other sex, flatter women for their powers of work and organisation, invite them to come and canvas for them at their elections, so that they may teach their electors how to vote, but when these weak women have done so, and have hoisted their candidates into the House, these men turn round and say, "Good-bye, thank you, we have no more need of you. We do not represent you, but those electors you created for us." Thus it is, that while our friends in the House bring forward Bills, Resolutions and Amendments, our watchful opponents are ever ready in fertile subtleties with means to frustrate them. Talking out, blocking bills, unexpected holidays, government absorptions of private members' days, all are made means of opposition to women's bills. The result of the whole Parliamentary work for the thirteen

years may be summed up in Punch's words, in "The
Essence of Parliament for 1891 "—" Business done—
Women's Rights men dished ! "

I myself was present in the Ladies' Gallery at the
second reading of Mr. Faithful Begg's Bill of 1897, and
heard the frivolities of Mr. Radcliffe Cooke and Mr.
Labouchere. I rejoiced in the unexpected majority of
71, a majority in every party of the House, and, with
Mrs. Elmy and Miss Busk, who sat beside me, I thought
that our troubles were over then. But 23rd June, the
day on which our bill had to go into Committee, was
absorbed by the Diamond Jubilee of Queen Victoria, and
on 7th July, to which it was postponed, another bill stood
in front of it. On that day Mr. Labouchere used the opportunity of dilating upon the Liberty of Verminous persons
to talk out the Bill of the Liberties of Womanhood.

It will always be talked out until it is made a
Government Bill ; it has been talked out again this
year, in the presence of an overwhelming majority who
wanted to divide, but the women met afterwards in
Exeter Hall, as Mr. Zangwill said, "to talk it in again."

In other directions they have not had a brilliant record
either. The Local Government Bill of 1894 confirmed
the rights of women as electors, and their eligibility as
Poor Law Guardians, and made them eligible as Parish
and as District Councillors. In 1896 the Poor Law
Guardian Bill for Ireland was passed, and in 1898 the
Irish Local Government Bill on the same lines as that
of England, so there was a new sphere opened to

philanthropic Irishwomen. In 1899 the London Government Act changed the system of Vestries to that of Borough Councils, which threw women out of the Vestries and excluded them from the Borough Councils. Women on the School Boards have been treated in the same way.

Meanwhile Factory Legislation goes on interfering with women's Freedom of Labour, without consulting them as to their needs, or making up to them for their losses.

All the facts up to 1902 (when her lamented death closed her work) are given in Miss Helen Blackburn's "Records of Women's Suffrage," and "Women under the Factory Acts," by Miss Blackburn and Miss Vynne.

Since then the conduct of a great war, undertaken to enfranchise the Uitlanders in another continent, has absorbed the time that might have been devoted to the interests of women, and made them feel bitterly that they are Uitlanders, indeed, in Britain, the land of their birth, not of their colonisation, but that no fatherland was arising in its might to protect their rights and enfranchise them.

Then came the change of Government, and our renewed hopes that as the Liberal Government of 1832 had disfranchised women, the Liberal Government of 1906 was to make all the amends in its power by confirming the application of Lord Brougham's Act to the Representation of the people's Acts.

Never had we had such a large majority pledged to

support us, never had we had so many apparent
opportunities, but we had again to learn that one
opponent in the House can outweigh many friends.
On the 19th May, 1906, the Prime Minister received
a deputation of 500 women, representing all classes,
from Peeress to Mill-girl; all interests in Literature,
Science, Manual Industry, Philanthropy, Temperance,
Morality and Religion; representative women were
allowed to state their case, but because of divided
counsels in the Cabinet, the only answer the Prime
Minister could give to all was "Patience!" Every
opportunity of having our bill passed has been frustrated,
and another great blot has fallen on a Liberal Government that has made all the nations of the earth wonder.
The women of the Social and Political Union, despairing
of success, attempted their appeal in an informal manner,
were attacked by mounted police, and many of them
dragged to prison, where they had to suffer punishments
and indignities meted out to hardened criminals. "How
long, O Lord, how long?" "Patience" has become a
crime.

What are we to do next? That, being only a private
individual, I cannot answer officially, but something
must be done, and something will be done. I know
that two difficulties are frequently imported into the
discussion, the difficulty of married women, and the
difficulty of Universal Suffrage. While I am quite aware
that married women, above all other classes of the
community, require and deserve the vote, still, when

we combine married women with widows and spinsters in one bill, we are asking the House to answer two questions at once, one that the disability of sex be removed, and the other that the disability of marriage be removed. I confess, I think it would have been much simpler had we secured the suffrage long ago, on a mere property basis, for widows and spinsters, and now were able to spend all our energies in framing a clear bill to enfranchise married women. For people will not understand that it is only proposed to enfranchise married women on the same terms as they are enfranchised in the Local Government Acts. The Statutes are not clear in their case as yet, and this indistinctness obscures the direct issues of the simple claim on the basis of the Statutes and the Franchises as they are.

Another difficulty is imported into the question by the desire of some to include in the bills for Women's enfranchisement that of all the yet unenfranchised men. Whatever men may privately think of Universal Suffrage, no one who has really and intelligently the interests of women at heart would desire to press it at the same time, for it is to clog the appeal to abolish the disability of sex for women, with a totally unconnected requirement to create a new franchise for a section of the other sex. The two separate demands would be better dealt with in two separate bills.

The more homogeneous and simple a bill is, the more likely it is to pass.

P

Though I cannot say what we are going to do next, I may emphasise the opinion that I have held all along, that we must give up all party politics, and work only for the *women's party*. What does party in a State mean, when half of the people are shut, by sex alone, out of its pale? What right has a man to call himself Liberal, when he denies the fundamental principle of Liberalism? What right has a man to call himself a Conservative, who does not conserve the fundamental basis of the English Constitution? We must only work for those who see clearly that Women's Enfranchisement is the greatest question in the whole country, and the most urgent need.

How can we make men see this? Some have suggested that all assessed women should refuse to pay their taxes. The misfortune is, that this will entail much trouble, worry and expense to the women, and very little to the House. The clogged wheels of Parliamentary procedure move but slowly through the ruts of London clay; the tax-gatherer comes and goes, as if he drove on a sleigh over smooth ice. His path is made clear before him, and behind there is protection.

Personally, I should advise that we should first make a unanimous appeal to be put on the Register through the application of Lord Brougham's Act to the Representation of the people's acts as they stand. This will give the Clerks at the Town Halls something to do and to think of. Of course we should fail at present, but then we could appeal. There is not a statement made in Chorlton *v.* Lings that cannot be controverted. While the case is *sub judice*, it would be legal, even at the present day, not to pay our taxes. In that we can be supported by the Statute (21 Edward I.), *De Tallagio non concedendo*, which every woman ought to learn by heart. Its main clauses are :—

c. 1. That no taxes be levied without assent of the representatives of those taxed.

c. 2. That no Royal officer "shall take any goods from any manner of persons without the good-will and assent of the party to whom the goods belong."

How can voteless women be said to give their assent, when their taxes are assessed, levied, and wrested from them? But this is only one suggestion. There are many paths leading towards the franchise, there *should be none leading from it.*

During the thirteen years we have lost many of our beloved leaders, but others have stepped forward to fill the ranks of the vanguard, for our cause is *alive.* The spirit of God has moved through the valley of dry bones, and a great army of living men and women have arisen to help. Encouragement comes from enfranchised peoples in the colonies, examples even from hide-bound Russia.

As yet there are *no British Freewomen*, but we know within our souls there are many about to be.

" And coming events cast their shadow before." Even

as I write, at the close of this Session, the Qualifications of Women (County and Borough Councils Bill, 1907) has become law.   In it is provided that women may be elected to County and Borough Councils, as Chairmen of County Councils and Mayors of Boroughs, but women who hold either of these latter offices shall not be *ex officio* Justices of the Peace, as male Chairmen or Mayors would be.   The Bill for England and Wales passed the House of Lords in its final form on Saturday, 24th August, and the Qualification of Women (County and Town Councils, Scotland) passed on Monday, 26th August.   The Royal assent was given to both Bills on Wednesday, 28th August, and they are therefore now *Acts of Parliament.*   In a circular letter of " The Women's Local Government Society," dated this month, it is stated, " As candidates for Town Councils, *only electors are eligible.*   Those single women and widows whose names are on the local Register are eligible, but no married women."   There remains therefore one great piece of work to be done before the reform is really completed.   Marriage (to a woman) must no longer be made a disgrace and a disability.   Surely it is reasonable to believe that the training of married women makes their counsel of special value to the State.   Men are uneasily beginning to feel that they cannot hope to keep "the First Commandment with promise," so long as they deliberately *dishonour their mothers* by classifying them with "idiots and criminals."

The passing of these two Acts will give an

unprecedented impulse to the completion of the enfranchisement of women, because, as I have shown in this
book, and perhaps even more fully in my little book,
" The Sphere of ' Man,' in relation to that of ' Woman '
in the Constitution," the Parliamentary franchise was the
right of *Burgesses* in the towns, as well as of *Freeholders*
in the counties, of either sex. The statements of judges
as to the natural and legal incapacity of women for
holding great offices and fulfilling great responsibilities
will be contravened in future, and lawyers need no
further obscure "statutes." In the hands of men is
placed at present a solemn responsibility. We have
faith that ere long they will awake to its meaning and
its importance, and without fear and without delay that
they will " Trust in God, and do the right."

When women have *fair-play*, then will the Sun of
Freedom shine on the old country.

THE END.

INDEX TO BRITISH FREEWOMEN

Q

Printed by Cowan & Co., Limited, Perth.

OPINIONS OF THE PRESS.

" THIS is the most complete story of the Women's suffrage question from the historical and constitutional point of view that has yet appeared. Mrs. Stopes shows us the true position of the movement, not as an isolated fact of to-day, but as the necessary outcome of a long series of changes, which have imperceptibly modified our institutions — changes to which the women's vote has become a necessary counter-balance and completion." — *Englishwoman's Review.*

" A spirited vindication of the political rights of women. This question is treated by the authoress historically and constitutionally, and the legal, political, and economic aspects are not neglected."— *Westminster Review.*

" Certainly not the least interesting and valuable of the volumes of the Social Science Series. It contains a collection of facts sifted out with much industry, and arranged with great care and skill."— *Scotsman.*

" Cordially to be welcomed."— *Yorkshire Post.*

" Mrs. Stopes has brought together a very large amount of out-of-the-way information regarding the position of women in civic and Parliamentary affairs in the early history of Great Britain, which bears on the questions of to-day."— *Dundee Advertiser.*

" A compilation of most interesting historical facts concerning the rights and privileges which women enjoyed in England, from the ancient British days to the seventeenth century."— *Lady.*

" Well worthy the attention of all interested in what Mrs. Stopes calls ' the greatest question of the day.'"— *Newcastle Chronicle.*

For EU product safety concerns, contact us at Calle de José Abascal, 56–1°,
28003 Madrid, Spain or eugpsr@cambridge.org.

www.ingramcontent.com/pod-product-compliance
Ingram Content Group UK Ltd.
Pitfield, Milton Keynes, MK11 3LW, UK
UKHW010341140625
459647UK00010B/751